the
mummy
coach

10 essential skills you
need to be a great mum

Lorraine Thomas

An Hachette UK Company
www.hachette.co.uk

First published in Great Britain in 2010 by Hamlyn,
a division of Octopus Publishing Group Ltd
2–4 Heron Quays, London E14 4JP
www.octopusbooks.co.uk

Lorraine Thomas asserts the moral right to be identified as
the author of this work

ISBN 978-0-600-61863-8

A CIP catalogue record for this book is available from the
British Library

Printed and bound in China

10 9 8 7 6 5 4 3 2 1

contents

introduction

*Being a mum is the most rewarding and challenging job you will ever do in your life – and it is **definitely** the most important. The stakes are very high. You are in a lifelong relationship with your son or daughter and you want to be the best mum you can.*

parents as pioneers

Children don't come with a set of instructions and as a mum you are a pioneer, charting new waters every day. Every day brings new adventures and new challenges as you constantly explore the exciting and ever-changing world of parenthood. It is a roller coaster ride that is both thrilling and scary – and every day is different and unpredictable. This is what makes being a mum such an adventure.

good relationships grow stronger when you nurture them

By reading this book, you are demonstrating just how committed you are to being a great mum. You are making the very positive decision to develop your skills and nurture your relationship with your children. This is a great decision for you and your family. If a relationship is to flourish and grow stronger, it needs time and energy invested in it. It needs working at – it doesn't just happen. This is especially true of the relationship between mums and their children.

every 10 minutes makes a difference

This book is for real mums who live in the real world – with a lot to think about and do – and finite reserves of energy. It is easy to dip into, with lots of quick, practical ideas to help you be a great parent. It is easy to read and, if you can find just 10 minutes a day, you will learn skills and strategies that will make a real difference in your own and your children's lives. The coaching activities are simple and practical – and easy for you to put into practice in your busy life. This is why they work and you will find that small, simple changes will bring about powerful results.

be the mum you want to be

It is important to read Chapter 1 first and Chapter 10 last, but the chapters in between can be read in any order – so you can use this book in the way that is most useful for you. Each chapter gives you the opportunity to rate yourself at a particular skill and set yourself specific targets. You will enjoy closing the gap between the mum you are now and the mum you want to be using the three simple skill-building steps in each chapter. Each step is full of practical activities that are easy for you to integrate into your hectic family life. It is ideal for busy mums and you can return to the book again and again to build your skills further.

find solutions to family problems

This book will also help you rise to family challenges and find solutions to problems you may be facing. Parent coaching is very practical and positive and this is why it works so powerfully with mums. Mums are fantastic practical problem-solvers. Parent coaching helps you break down the big picture into manageable chunks and take simple steps to find a solution that works for you and your family.

In this book, there are plenty of examples to set you thinking – but your own ideas will always be better than the ones you read. You are on a unique personal journey, so ultimately it is up to you to decide on an action plan that is right for you. You may find it helpful to reserve a special notebook for your thoughts, feelings, goals and successes. You can put in the dates and, when you look back, you will see just how much you have achieved on your journey.

you are the expert

Being a mum is an unpredictable adventure. Each chapter in this book will take you forward on that journey. You will be acknowledging the skills and qualities that you have already and developing new tools and techniques to use along the way.

You are the expert on your family – and it is important to believe in yourself. I am not here to push you or pull you in a particular direction. I am here to walk with you every step of the way as you head towards the destination that you have chosen. And as mums, that is what we want to do with our children too. We don't want to push or pull them; we want to walk with them on their journey towards independence and adulthood. We want to be there for them – always.

On page 119, you will find a contract for you to sign. It marks your achievement in completing the journey and is a significant milestone in your development as a mum.

believe in yourself

Sometimes, as a mum, you may feel that you are stuck where you are. You stand still, looking at the ground, rather than moving forward with your eye on your chosen destination. You are too busy fire-fighting and trying to cope with the normal challenges of daily family life to think about doing things differently. But our journey isn't about standing still. It is about taking action and moving forward one step at a time. So let us do it. It is time for you to set your sights on your goal – and to enjoy your journey there.

There is only one thing you need to make sure you have before you take your first step – self-belief. You have a great deal to be proud of. As a mum you achieve a huge amount every hour of every day. It is so important to acknowledge everything you achieve and the many great skills and qualities you already have. If you believe in yourself, you will achieve great things – and so will your children.

I am my child's number 1 role model

Being a mum is an amazing and huge responsibility. You are in a life-long relationship with your son or daughter and it is unique. You hold your child's hands for a short time – and their hearts forever. You are your child's most important and powerful role model – and you always will be. As they grow older and are exposed to a wide range of different influences, you will always remain the most significant influence in their lives.

▶ You will have a **powerful and positive effect** on your child's life and the adult that they will become

▶ You will be **fulfilled** because you are enjoying being the mum you want to be

▶ You will have a **happy child** with **strong self-belief**

you hold the key to your child's future

It is essential to recognize that you are the most important person in your child's life. The role model you provide for your child on a daily basis has a huge and direct impact. As a mum, everything you say and do colours the world they grow up in. It affects the way they behave and their view of life. It makes a difference to the way they develop and the adults they become.

Close your eyes and focus on your child's smiling face and feel their excitement for life and the love they have for you. Now focus on yourself as a mum. Don't clutter your mind with any negatives – the things you don't do or could do better. What kind of a mum do you want to be to your child?

As a mum, you are the most important person in your child's life. You are the only person who knows what kind of mum you want to be – and you are the only person who can make it happen.

enjoy the responsibility

You are your child's most important role model – and you always will be. That is an immense responsibility. When you have a family, it is a good time to get up close and personal and take a look at yourself. When you look closely, you will probably find things you are really proud of – and a few bad habits you would like to break.

Becoming a mum gives you the opportunity to make decisions about the kind of role model you want to be. One of the great things about having a child is that it motivates you to reassess your priorities. It is a good time to recognize what you do well and identify some specific areas you would like to work on. It is a time to reflect and set some targets that will benefit you and the whole family.

close the gap

There is no such thing as a perfect parent and it is important not to give yourself the impossible task of trying to be one. One of the very best things you can do when it comes to being a role model is to recognize what you do well and to celebrate it and build on it. If you do that, your child will do the same. This chapter is about spending a few minutes setting some specific goals for yourself as a role model and taking small steps to start to close the gap between the mum you are now and the mum you want to be.

human 'being' or human 'doing'?

Your child will 'catch' your values, beliefs and habits from what you do every day. When it comes to being a powerful positive role model, it is about what you **do** in family life.

We are all human beings, but when it comes to being a mum, it is important to focus not just on **being** but also on **doing**. For your son or daughter, your actions will always speak louder and more powerfully than your words. So stop doing anything you don't want to see your child doing and commit to doing what you want to see them doing. One great habit you can get into is taking a few minutes each day to focus on yourself and what you want to achieve – and to do it.

little changes get powerful results

What your child sees you doing – not just talking about doing – they will do too. Your child will follow in your pioneering footsteps with vision, commitment, positive attitude, energy, strength and belief in themselves.

breaking bad habits

1

Our children catch our bad habits in the same way they catch our good habits. Now is a good time to focus on any bad habits you want to break.

2

All bad habits can be broken with a great incentive – and having children is the best incentive in the world.

3

It is often the smallest changes that have the greatest impact.

get to know yourself

These activities will help you to focus on your role as a mum in a very specific and powerful way. You are assessing where you are today and making decisions about the kind of mum you want to be. By being clear about your goal and the direction you want to move in, you are taking the first step to making it happen.

1 your role-model rating

There will be lots of very positive things that you do now that make you a great role model to your son or daughter. **Think about some of the powerful ways in which you set a great example,** perhaps in an area of your own life.

The examples below will give you some ideas to get you started. **Tick those that apply to you but feel free to add you own ideas:**

☐ I rise to challenges

☐ I live life to the full

☐ I enjoy doing something new

☐ I count my blessings

☐ I enjoy having fun

☐ I am helpful to others

☐ I sit down to eat my meals

☐ I have a relaxing bedtime routine

☐ I enjoy exercise, such as walking and swimming

☐ I have regular dental check-ups

Now give yourself a role-model rating on a scale of 1 to 10 – where 10 indicates an excellent role model and a mark of 2 or 3 indicates that you do well in some areas but there are changes you would like to make.

Don't worry if you give yourself a low score. It is helpful because it means you are being honest and recognizing that there are some areas to work on.

2 the role-model quiz

Look at the statements below. They describe some of the ways in which you can be a positive and powerful role model to your child. Focus on each 'I am' statement and decide how you would describe your performance in each case: A – Strong; B – OK; C – Weak.

Role model skill	A	B	C
I am positive about discipline and setting boundaries	☐	☐	☐
I am a calm mum	☐	☐	☐
I am a great listener	☐	☐	☐
I am a fun mum not a frantic mum	☐	☐	☐
I am a strong stress manager	☐	☐	☐
I am a confidence-booster	☐	☐	☐
I am a motivating team leader	☐	☐	☐
I am a feel good mum not a feel guilty mum	☐	☐	☐
I am the mum I want to be	☐	☐	☐

believe in yourself

Focus on your positive qualities and it will help to give you the confidence to move forward in the areas you find more challenging.

say your thoughts out loud

If you say your thoughts out loud to yourself or somebody else, they instantly become more powerful than just thinking them or writing them down. Every time you say your affirmation, you will take another step towards your goal.

3 the 24-hour role-model challenge

Choose one statement that you would like to focus on over the next 24 hours and make positive changes so that you can be an even better role model than you are already. It may be an area where you do well already but would like to get even better. Or it may be an area where you think you have lots of room for improvement. Make this area your priority. Don't try to do everything at once.

Write down the statement you have chosen, for example, I am a 'fun mum' not a 'frantic mum' and stick it up where you can't fail to miss it.

say your written 'I am' affirmation out loud

▶ First thing in the morning when you get up

▶ Last thing at night before you go to sleep

▶ As often as you can in between

role models make a difference

As your child's role model, you have a direct impact on their lives. Take a few minutes now to focus on your son or daughter and some of the specific skills and qualities and behaviours he or she displays.

1 the behaviour quiz

Now focus on your child. **Take a look at the statements below** and decide how often they apply to your child:
A – Usually; B – Rarely.

My child's qualities and skills	A	B
My child is calm	☐	☐
My child is positive about discipline and responds well to boundaries	☐	☐
My child is a great listener	☐	☐
My child is fun	☐	☐
My child manages stress well	☐	☐
My child is confident	☐	☐
My child is a motivated member of the family team	☐	☐
My child feels good about himself	☐	☐
Total out of 8	☐	☐

how did you score?

Mostly As You are a good and positive role model. Your child is displaying these behaviours more often than not and is definitely moving in the right direction. The more you work on these areas in your own life, the greater impact it will have on your child.

Mostly Bs You have identified specific areas where it would be helpful for you to support your child. The most powerful way to do this is to work on these areas in your own life and be the best role model you can be for your child.

2 go for goal!

Think about the areas where you might help your child most effectively by providing a strong role model. Remember this is about how **you** behave, not just with your children but with everyone.

Then choose **one area** where you would like to help your child to make **positive changes**, write it down and **make it your priority**. The table below gives some examples of what you could do.

If you don't have a goal, you are never going to achieve it. The more specific you are about the details of the mum you want to be, the easier you will find it to achieve your goal. Specific goals are easier to achieve than general ones – both for you and your child.

Areas needing help	Role model priority
Your child is rarely calm	Commit to staying calm today by counting to three before saying anything you will later regret – to your child, husband or mother-in-law
Your child is nearly always calm	Look out for the occasional triggers that lead to tantrums (yours and your child's) and deal with them before you start to shout
Your child rarely listens well	Sit down for at least 10 minutes today and really listen to what your child is talking to you about and give him your full attention
Your child rarely feels good about himself	Recognize what you do well as a mum and talk to your child about what you love about him

motivating mum
Be clear about what is a priority for you and believe that you can do it. Focus on the difference it will make to you and your family when you achieve it. Understand your motivation. The stronger your motivation and the more you want to do something, the more you will **do** to make it happen.

3 your own inspirations

As an adult, you will have been inspired by many role models over the years. If you were to pick **one person** who has been the most important and positive role model in your life, who would you choose? Write his or her name in the large box below.

Next **consider what three specific positive skills or qualities** they demonstrate that inspire you to want to be like them in some way. Write these in the smaller boxes. For example:

my most important role model is

> my mum

> She is always there for me

> She is relaxed about housework and knows it is not important

> She is positive and always sees the bright side of life

By focusing specifically on what you admire in other people, you will be motivating yourself to take a step towards boosting that skill or quality in yourself.

values are the foundation of family life

Having a child is a good time to take a fresh look at what is important to you and how you want your family to live. It is a great opportunity to make sure your values are good enough to pass on. Understanding and living common values are the foundation of a happy family life.

1 prioritize your values

Your values make you who you are. They indicate what is really important to you and determine how you want to live your life. As a mum, the more you 'live' your values, the more powerful and positive a role model you will be.

Think about the values that are important to you. Some examples of the values that mums pass on are listed below, but you probably have more ideas of your own. Number the boxes that apply to you in order of priority.

- [ ] Compassion
- [ ] Courage
- [ ] Fairness
- [ ] Healthy living
- [ ] Honesty
- [ ] Loving
- [ ] Optimism
- [ ] Respect and consideration for others
- [ ] Responsibility for actions
- [ ] Security
- [ ] Sense of adventure
- [ ] Sense of fun
- [ ] Spirituality
- [ ] Wisdom

2 boost your values

The more you live your own values and the more you are the mum you want to be, the happier you and your family will be.

The tell-tale signs of a mum who is living her values are:
► She is happy and motivated
► She is positive and energized
► She is a great role model

The tell-tale signs of a mum who is not living her values are:
► She is unhappy and demotivated
► She is negative and tired
► She is not a great role model.

You are the beating heart of your family. **Draw a large heart and choose three values** that you think are the most important ones for you to pass on to your child – such as 'love', 'optimism' and 'honesty' – and write them on your heart. Then add examples of what **you** can do to demonstrate each of these values.

This activity will help to stop you taking your values for granted. It is also an opportunity to talk to your child about a subject that is fundamental to family life, but may be rarely mentioned.

value-boosting plan
► **Put your heart somewhere very visible** as a constant reminder of what really matters.
► **Talk to your child** about what makes your words so important to you. Do this even if your child is too small to reply.
► **Identify specific things you do or can do** to demonstrate that value. Write them down on the heart chart to remind you to **do** them. Your child may have some ideas too.

This is a great way for your child to really get to know you and what makes you tick. And it will help them to realize that you are constantly working at being the best mum you can be for them.

teaching by example
Your values are 'caught' by your child not 'taught' to them, so remember that your actions will always speak louder than your words.

3 make family values fun

Choose one of the values on your heart chart and have fun catching your child 'red-handed' demonstrating that value. When you do see them 'living that family value', praise them and explain what you like about what they are doing. You can give them a sticker if you want to.

If they are old enough, encourage them to catch you 'red-handed' in exactly the same way. Make it a game. Turn it into family fun and it will increase their understanding. It will raise their awareness and help raise your own game.

You have taken time to focus on your values. The more you live your values, the more direction your life will have and the greater role model you will be.

troubleshooting

Now that you are a mum, you want to be fitter and have more energy for your child. Your lifestyle is unhealthy and after a stressful day at work, comfort food and a drink may be a much more attractive option than dragging yourself to the gym.

▶ You have made the most important step by deciding you want to change your lifestyle. Your motivation for getting healthy is strong, so keep the benefits to you and your child at the top of your mind.

▶ Take things a day at a time. Focus on your healthy habits, not your unhealthy habits. Feel good about yourself each time you drink a glass of water or eat a piece of fruit. Set yourself one positive health target for each day. Make it simple and easy, such as taking the stairs instead of the lift, and enjoy doing it.

▶ Stock up on delicious and nutritious snacks. By developing healthy eating habits yourself, your child will learn to develop them too. Think yourself healthy by being positive about life. Optimists have more energy than pessimists. And make the most of your own personal trainer – your child. Being a mum is the perfect way to boost your fun and fitness levels.

You have separated from your partner and are both struggling to help your child cope with this. You are also worried because they won't have dad as a male role model living at home.

▶ Your feelings are natural. It is really difficult when a relationship breaks down and children are involved. Keep strong. By dealing with this challenging situation positively, you will have a significant impact on your child.

▶ Encourage your child to talk to you and your partner about their feelings and talk to them about how you feel. What is most important now is to make sure they know that you both love them and are there for them. Children ask tough questions, so be prepared for these. Decide together in advance what you want to say. You may both have difficult feelings to wrestle with – but commit to work as a team to help your child through this. You can't change what has happened, but you can still give them a happy and secure childhood.

▶ Dad will always be an important role model, even if he only sees his child at weekends. Encourage regular contact during the week – by phone, by email or by texting. Make sure your child comes into contact with lots of other positive male role models through family and friends.

Your son's best friend gets money or a toy as a reward for doing his homework. Your child thinks he should too. You really don't want to go down that road but feel under pressure to do it.

▶ Don't do it. Be the mum you want to be – not the mum you feel under pressure to be. Believe in the values that are important to you and stick to them.

▶ Your child won't benefit from being 'paid' for doing his homework and you can easily end up spending money that you can't afford. If you want to give him an occasional 'treat' for working hard, make sure it is just that and help him to appreciate it, not take it for granted.

▶ Stay calm and explain the positive reasons for your decision. We all struggle with saying 'No'. But if you give your child something every time they ask, you are teaching them that the way to get what they want is to demand it. Learning the values of things in life – rather than the cost – is a vital lesson that they will appreciate later.

I am positive about discipline

As a mum, you will already have developed strong skills when it comes to teaching your child about discipline and setting – and sticking to – boundaries. You learn this on the job and you probably take many of your achievements for granted. However, it is very normal for mums to focus on areas of family life that aren't quite going according to plan. Sometimes the challenges can seem so overwhelming that you forget your strengths and what is going well.

▶Discipline and boundaries create a **positive framework** within which your child can develop

▶Boundaries help your child to **know where they stand** and helps them to feel secure and valued

▶Boundaries show that **you care about your child** and what they are doing

discipline isn't the same as punishment

note to self

Explain to my child what I want them to do instead of what I don't want them to do. Children find positive statements much easier to process than negative ones.

When it comes to discipline, it is easy to fall into the trap of thinking of 'discipline' in negative terms and meaning the same as 'punishment'. When you think of yourself as having to exercise discipline, you may feel it is a negative role and will usually lead to you telling off your child or punishing them. This is stressful for both you and your family.

Discipline actually has a very positive meaning and is very different from 'punishment'. Discipline provides a framework within which our children can grow and flourish.

The word discipline comes from a Latin word, meaning teaching. As a mum, you teach your child what is important in life, to develop a zest for living and help them to embrace their exciting journey into adulthood. Your child is learning life's most important lessons from you. That is an awesome responsibility. Everything you say or do will influence your child and colour the world they grow up in. As their teacher, every day is a new opportunity to make a positive difference in their lives.

Aim for connection with your child – not perfection. Connecting with your son or daughter will be your most powerful and effective achievement. The stronger your connection, the more successful you will be in family discipline and setting boundaries that work. Don't try to be the perfect mum or have the perfect child because neither exists. Believe in yourself and acknowledge what you do well already.

successful discipline = connection not perfection

we all need boundaries

Setting boundaries is an essential part of discipline. It doesn't matter if we are a toddler or an adult. We all feel much happier when we have boundaries in our lives.

As a mum, you will know just how important boundaries are – and the stress and chaos caused when they are not there. Setting a boundary is a very positive thing to do. They give us an essential framework for living.

all children will flex their muscles

You know just how tough it can be to get your son or daughter to stick to the boundaries that you set. You will also know how difficult it can be for you to stand your ground without losing your calmness, especially if you are feeling tired or stressed, or under pressure to meet a deadline.

All children will flex their muscles and try to push the boundaries. This is normal behaviour. But they would be lost if the boundaries weren't there. This can happen at any time – refusing to get dressed or stop watching TV, refusing to share or go to bed. Pushing the boundaries is a normal part of growing up and learning to be independent.

celebrate your successes

Think about what works well for your family and the boundaries that you have made part of family life. There will be many of these and you may take them for granted. Identify one successful boundary and focus on the positive difference it makes to your family.

It is important that you appreciate your strengths. Your child learns from you. If you are constantly putting yourself down, they are more likely to feel negative about themselves. If you get into the habit of acknowledging the things that you do well, they are more likely to do the same for themselves.

the golden rules for setting successful boundaries

1
Focus on one boundary at a time.

2
Communicate it positively, explaining the benefits to all the family.

3
Involve your children in setting the boundary – they will be much more likely to keep to it.

4
Be committed to making it work and you will be able to make it happen.

identify your strengths

As a mum, you will already be doing a lot of things well when it comes to positive discipline and setting boundaries. Mums always give themselves a hard time. They are great at telling themselves what they didn't do, should have done, or wished they had done differently. They are not so good at celebrating their achievements – and as a mum you achieve a huge amount on a daily basis.

1 do you set a good example?

How good are you at keeping to boundaries in your own life? For example:

▶ Do you stick to them – or do you find reasons to 'push them just this once'?

▶ Do you leave work on time?

▶ Do you control your housework or does it control you?

▶ Do you create valuable 'me' time to recharge your batteries?

If you want your child to learn to keep boundaries, make sure you are doing it too.

be positive not negative
Some parents worry about appearing too strict and the resentment that setting and enforcing rules may cause. If you stop thinking about boundaries in a negative way, your child is more likely to as well.

2 your commitment rating

How committed are you to making your boundaries work? **Give yourself a rating on a scale of 1 to 10** – where 1 means Not very committed and 10 means Extremely committed.

If you have given yourself a rating of 8 or above you will make it happen. If you have given yourself a rating of 7 you probably aren't sufficiently committed to see them through.

3 the boundary setting quiz

Take a look at the statements below. Each identifies a specific skill that helps you to be effective in creating family discipline and setting boundaries. For each statement, decide whether you are: A Strong; B OK; C Definitely need to improve.

Boundary setting skill	A	B	C
I set specific boundaries	☐	☐	☐
I communicate the positive reasons for the boundary	☐	☐	☐
I involve my child in setting the boundary	☐	☐	☐
I am consistent when implementing boundaries	☐	☐	☐
I am good at motivating my child to keep within the boundary	☐	☐	☐
I am willing to negotiate over some boundaries	☐	☐	☐
I tell my child what I want him to do rather than what I don't want him to do	☐	☐	☐
I am good at giving my child specific praise for keeping within a boundary	☐	☐	☐

how did you score?

Mostly As Excellent – you are a skilled disciplinarian and great at boundary-setting.

Mostly Bs You are performing well in important areas and ready to take your game to the next level.

Mostly Cs You have lots of specific areas to work on. It is good to have identified these.

Choose one area that you would like to focus on over the next 24 hours. It may be one where you feel there is room for improvement – or it may be one that you are good at already but want to get even better.

By focusing on one particular area of your discipline and boundary-setting skills, you are making a decision and turning it into a priority.

skill builder

create boundaries that work

As a mum, the key to setting successful boundaries is in your hands – not your child's. Once you have chosen your boundaries it is vital that you commit yourself to making them work.

1 identify your family hotspots

Take a look at the list below, which shows the main areas that mums identify as most stressful when it comes to making boundaries work.

- ☐ Early mornings
- ☐ Mealtimes
- ☐ Behaviour in public
- ☐ TV habits
- ☐ Computer/video games
- ☐ Tantrums
- ☐ Homework
- ☐ Bedtimes
- ☐ Pressure to spend money
- ☐ Other

Identify one area you want to focus on. You may have set a boundary and let it slip. Or you may never have got around to it in the first place – there is always so much to do!

take one thing at a time

If you try to do everything at once, you are likely to end up doing nothing. By focusing on one particular area of family life and making that your priority, you are more likely to succeed.

2 write a clear and positive message

Focus on the boundary you want to create and write it down. Make it as specific as you possibly can. The clearer you are about what you want to happen, the easier it will be to get the message across to your family.

Word it in a positive way. Identify what you want your child to do instead of what you don't want them to do.

don't write

▶ I want to stop Jane watching so much TV

▶ I want Harry to stop eating so many sweets

▶ I don't want to shout at Dan when he won't do what he is told

do write

▶ I am happy for Jane to watch 30 minutes of TV each day

▶ I want Harry to eat five portions of fruit and vegetables each day

▶ I want to be calm and in control when Dan won't do what he is told

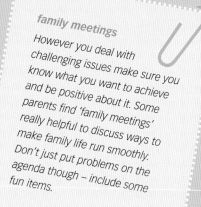

family meetings

However you deal with challenging issues make sure you know what you want to achieve and be positive about it. Some parents find 'family meetings' really helpful to discuss ways to make family life run smoothly. Don't just put problems on the agenda though – include some fun items.

3 the eight-step boundary action plan

By taking **one step at a time** you will reach achieve your goal.

1 Believe in yourself.

2 Write down the main benefit to you of making this boundary work.

3 Write down the biggest benefit to your child of making this boundary work.

4 Check that the boundary is described in positive language.

5 Check that it is specific and realistic. See it through your child's eyes and make any adjustments that may help you both.

6 When you are calm, explain what you want your child to do – instead of what you don't want them to do.

7 Ask them for their feedback and ideas and use them if you can.

8 Write the boundary out in large letters and put it where it can be easily seen.

keep to your boundaries

Keeping to your boundaries is where the real challenge lies. Your child may do what they can to push them – but if you are committed to play by your rules, not theirs, they will soon learn that you mean business.

1 catch them 'red-handed' being good

The best way to discipline your child is by giving them positive attention. Praise will shape their behaviour more effectively than negative attention.

Specific praise is much more powerful than general praise. If your child knows exactly what it is that they have done well and you praise them for it, they are much more likely to do it again.

Go out of your way to catch your child behaving well today – and praise them. It may help to give them stars or stickers.

attention seeking

When you tell your child off, you are still giving them the attention they crave. It may be negative but it is still attention. You may think you are making your point to get what you want, but actually they are getting what they want.

2 stand your ground

Standing your ground when your child is pushing a boundary is one of the toughest times you face as a mum. It is a time when all your best intentions can go out of the window and you are tempted to give in 'just this once'. Don't. Recognize that you have the skills and strength to rise to whatever challenge family life throws at you.

remember the ABC – Always Be Consistent

Every child will have a go at stepping over the line. It is a normal part of growing up and becoming independent. Children want to know if their mum really means business or if they can use their battle skills to wear her down.

It is tough to be consistent when you are tired or stressed. But it is important to **have an action plan** – one that you have thought about and committed to when you were calm, not one that you create on the spur of the moment.

Decide in advance how you will respond if a child pushes a boundary. Focus on what is important and ignore what is not. If the child deliberately breaks a rule, apply a fair consequence. If you are consistent, your child will receive a clear message and find keeping the boundary easier.

the 7-day 'just this once' challenge
Commit to making your child keep to your boundary for 7 days – without giving in 'just this once' – and you will make it work. If you are tempted to give in, remember this is a short-term fix and you will be making life harder for yourself in the long run. Take it one day at a time and you can make it happen.

lose a battle but win the war
Conflict is inevitable in normal family life. Be clear about which boundaries are negotiable and which ones aren't. Listen to what your child has to say and be prepared to negotiate. It is important that all of you learn to give and take.

3 what have you taught your disciples today?

When a mum climbs into bed at the end of a busy day, her mind is often full of things that stop her getting a good night's sleep. If you are going to be the best mum you can be – positive, motivated and energetic – you need your rest.

Resist the temptation to think about what you found stressful during the day. Instead, spend a few minutes thinking about **what you did well** today as a mum (there will be many things) – and **one valuable lesson** that you taught your little 'disciple'. Often the most valuable lessons that mums and their children learn about discipline come out of the challenges that they have risen to.

troubleshooting

Your son is only 4 years old, but he already rules the TV remote control in your house. You end up letting him watch much more TV than you want him to because you can't face the tantrums when you turn it off – especially at mealtimes.

▶ You are not alone. It is children who wield the TV remote control in most homes – and they know just which buttons to press to put you under pressure!

▶ Start by taking a close look at your own TV habits. If you want your child to cut down on the amount of television he watches, set an example and cut down yourself.

▶ By giving in to your child, you are sending the message that, if he stamps her feet long enough, he will get what he wants. Decide when you want him to watch TV and when you don't, and stick to it. Keep the times before bed and before meals as TV-free zones.

▶ Challenge yourself to switch the TV off for 24 hours. Prove to yourself and your child that the world doesn't stop when the TV is off!

▶ It is easy to let the TV room become the centre of the family universe. Make sure your child knows that this is not the case. Have fun with him in other rooms. Build a den in his bedroom, let him cook in the kitchen or take longer having fun giving him a bath.

Night times are a nightmare for you because your children don't want to go to bed. They complain that their friends can stay up longer than they can and you are letting their bedtime get later and later. It means you have no time to yourself in the evening – and they are tired when they wake up.

▶ Trying to push the bedtime boundary is normal behaviour. However, if you give in to your children's demands, the whole family will suffer. You and your partner need to have some child-free time and your children need a good night's sleep.

▶ It is important to decide on the routine that you want your children to follow – and to stick to it for at least 7 days initially. Your children need to know where they stand. Play by your rules not theirs.

▶ Be clear about your goal by writing down the schedule with the specific time you want them to be in their bedrooms and at what time you want the lights switched off. Communicate this to them positively. Instead of saying, 'because I say so', explain the positive reasons for your decision.

▶ Allow some time for you to share a book or chat to them in their bedrooms. Give them some choices about what winding-down activity they would like to do before they go to sleep.

You and your partner have different ideas about being parents and often disagree about what to do when your children are misbehaving. He shouts much more than you do and uses ultimatums. You want him to be a calmer dad but don't know how to get him to change.

▶ When couples have children, they often find they have very different ideas about parenting. You need to work as a team. Your children need clear and consistent messages from both of you about how you want them to behave. What you want to avoid at all costs is arguing in front of them over discipline issues.

▶ Talk to your partner when you are both feeling positive and relaxed. Acknowledge what your partner does well as a dad. Be positive about your reasons for wanting him to stay calmer. This will help all of you – and especially your partner – feel less stressed and enjoy being a family.

▶ Praise your partner when he handles challenging situations calmly. It is really tough to keep your cool when your children are playing up and it takes practice and commitment.

▶ Different does not necessarily mean opposing and it is good to have a range of views sometimes. Identify the areas in which you need to agree and the areas where debate is a healthy option.

I am a calm mum

It happens to every mum. One moment you are on top of the world. You are having fun. You are calm. But suddenly, without warning, you are transformed from the practically perfect Mary Poppins into the wicked White Witch of Narnia in less time than it takes to say Winnie-the-Pooh! You can't even remember why. There was no major incident – no drawing on the plasma TV or putting the mobile telephone down the toilet. But suddenly you snap. You shout and your child shouts back. They stamp their feet and you do too. Most mums lose their sense of calm in challenging situations. Welcome to the world of parent tantrums.

▶ If you **shout** to get what you want, your child will learn to do the same

▶ If you are **calm** when dealing with challenging situations, your child will develop a sense of calm too

▶ You will cut your whole family's stress levels

parent tantrums are normal

We all know that children have tantrums – and most parents say that they have them too. It is often the little things that can bring out the worst in us and small incidents can escalate into major wars.

facts about parent tantrums

1 10 out of 10 mums say they want to feel calmer

2 9 out of 10 mums say they shout at their children and feel guilty

3 9 out of 10 mums say they are negative and say things they regret later

Most mums say that mornings and evenings are the times when they find it most difficult to keep their sense of calm. It is easy to understand why. In the morning, lots of families are up against deadlines and this puts pressure on everyone. In the evening, mums and children are often tired after a busy day and it is much harder to be calm when your energy levels are low.

your tantrums are about you – not your child

The majority of parents have tantrums at one time or another. They are just as natural as children's tantrums. Children throw tantrums because they are bored, hungry, tired, asserting their independence or wanting your attention. Their tantrums are about them – they aren't about you. When they throw a tantrum, they want to tell you something about how they are feeling.

In just the same way, your parent tantrums aren't really about them. It is about you and the way you are responding to a difficult situation.

Don't take what your child says or does personally. They are on an exciting – but tough and often confusing journey from childhood to adulthood. It is normal to have tantrums and push boundaries. It is part of their growing up – and you growing as a parent.

you are in the driving seat – not your child

You are the only person who can help **you** to calm down. You may feel that it is your child who is responsible for making you lose control, so that you end up shouting or saying things you regret later. They know what buttons to press and what to say to send you over the edge. But you can't wave a magic wand over your child and change them. You are the only person who can help yourself to stay calm and in control. By changing the way you respond to your child, you will also bring about positive changes in their behaviour.

cut noise and boost calm

Every family home is full of noise – the TV is on although no one is really watching, the computer is printing, the phone is ringing, the play station is blaring at full blast. It can seem as though your home has no volume control – and that is all without any of you opening your mouths.

Noise is stressful. Quiet is calming. Have at least one evening every week when you have a noise detox. **Switch off the TV, the computer and the video and enjoy the peace – and the opportunity to talk to your child.**

you are calmer than you think

A Parent Coaching Academy survey shows that most mums are calm for 90 per cent of the time and not calm for 10 per cent of the time. You probably are too. It is just that you focus on the stressful times when your child is being challenging and you aren't being the mum you want to be. It may feel as though you are calm for 10 per cent of the time and not calm for 90 per cent of the time – but the opposite is likely to be true.

take control

You are the only person who can create a calmer you. So get into the driving seat and take control. Prepare for a sometimes bumpy but always interesting and unpredictable ride. Take each day as an opportunity to move from where you are today towards the calmer mum you want to be.

1 the parent tantrum quiz

Look at the statements below to find out what you are doing well already when it comes to keeping calm – and what you want to work on. Think about what you have felt or done over the past 24 hours. Score 3 marks for A – Often; 2 marks for B – Sometimes; and 1 mark for C – Rarely.

Parent tantrum signs	A	B	C
I felt signs of physical tension	☐	☐	☐
I shouted to get what I wanted	☐	☐	☐
I said things I would not have said if I had felt calm	☐	☐	☐
I felt my child was in control – not me	☐	☐	☐
I acted as if I was my child's age	☐	☐	☐
I spent more time telling my child off than telling them what they did well	☐	☐	☐
I made a threat to make my child behave but didn't carry it out	☐	☐	☐
I spent more time telling my child what not to do rather than what to do	☐	☐	☐
I made negative personal remarks about my child	☐	☐	☐
I experienced feelings of guilt about being negative with my child	☐	☐	☐

how did you score?

26–30 Your child is in control. Life is too short to feel this stressed. It is time to take action.

16–25 You are responding well to challenges and have the potential to be a very calm mum.

10–15 You are a powerful role model. You can stay calm in challenging situations and you have parent tantrums under control.

2 resolve to be calm

Knowing you are the person who can help you calm down is liberating. It is within your control – not your child's. It may not always seem like it, but you are in the driving seat. It is easy to feel calm when everything is going well in family life. It is really tough to do it when you are tired or stressed or your child is being particularly challenging. **Focus now on what a difference it would make to you and to your family if you could feel calmer,** especially at these difficult times.

To move from where you are today to the calm mum you want to be takes:

▶ Commitment

▶ A positive attitude

▶ Energy

▶ Strength

▶ Belief in yourself

This is tough. You really have to want to do it to make it happen. Sign the calm contract below. By doing this, you are recognizing that this is going to be a real challenge – and you are rising to it.

calm contract

I am strong.

I am energetic.

I am positive.

I believe in myself.

I am committed to being a calmer mum.

Signature...

Date...

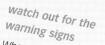

watch out for the warning signs

When you begin to feel your calm levels dipping, deal with it before you sink any further. You are the expert on you and your family situation. Your gut instinct is a great one, so use it.

3 how to stay calm

The first step to feeling calmer is to **believe in yourself and your abilities to handle challenging situations well.** Dealing with this is an opportunity for you to develop your skills and grow as a parent, to be a positive role model – and to be the mum you want to be.

Try this exercise:

▶ Close your eyes and count to 10

▶ Visualize a colour that helps you to relax

▶ Take 10 deep breaths. Focus on each breath as you take it

▶ Feel each breath filling you with a sense of calm

Now say to yourself – **I can be calm and handle challenging situations well.** If you believe you can – you will. If you believe you can't, you will be proved absolutely right.

calm boosters

Staying calm doesn't just happen. It is like lots of things about being a mum – you need to work at it on a daily basis. But if you practise, you can boost your sense of calm, especially in potentially stressful situations.

1 use tone not volume

When you are faced with children being difficult, it is easy to understand why you can end up shouting. You ask them to do something – it doesn't happen. You raise your voice – so do they. They shout – you shout louder.

turn down your volume

▶ Instead of shouting, lower the tone of your voice

▶ Get down to your child's level and look them in the eye

▶ Show your child that you are committed and mean business

note to self

Changing the way I use my voice will help me to stay calm. Shouting will not help me or my child. When I raise my voice or shout, I just feel more stressed and less calm. I will be much more effective – and much less stressed – by using tone instead of volume.

Your children seem determined to make your weekly shop a nightmare. They start playing up and arguing as soon as you get into the supermarket and you end up shouting as well.

▶ Every parent knows what it is like to experience supermarket trolley rage. It can bring out the very worst in you and your children. And a tantrum – yours or theirs – is always much more stressful when it happens in public.

▶ Remember that most other shoppers aren't judging you. They are more likely to be sympathizing because they have been there too.

▶ Stay strong. If you end up out of control – screaming at a tin of baked beans or at your children – that is just what your children will learn to do. If you are calm and relaxed, they will take their lead from you.

▶ Aim to shop when the supermarket isn't too busy and when your children are well-fed and relaxed. Change your perspective. Instead of aiming to do your shopping as quickly as you can, allow a little extra time to enjoy it. The shopping will take longer, but it will certainly be less stressful. It may help to get your children involved in the shopping.

▶ Make life easier by buying basic food shopping online.

Your mealtimes are mayhem. Your toddler daughter is determined to make your life difficult – and to create as much mess as possible. She refuses to eat and you end up stressed.

▶ Every mum knows how stressful mealtimes can be and how easily minor food battles can escalate into full-blown wars. It is a phase that all toddlers go through. If you want to cut your stress levels, take control and start playing the meal game by your rules – not hers.

▶ Relax and stop rushing. If you are stressed, your toddler will be stressed as well. Make mealtimes fun so that you both look forward to them. Aim to enjoy – not to endure. Make the time before eating a 'TV free' zone and encourage your toddler to help you with the meal instead.

▶ Toddlers' mealtimes are messy because they are learning new skills and becoming independent – do you remember eating your first plate of spaghetti? Don't force them to eat. 'No' is a word that a toddler loves as it always gets your attention. Ignore bad behaviour and praise her for eating well.

▶ Show your toddler that you value mealtimes. Don't load the washing machine or empty the dishwasher while she is eating. Sit down and eat with her.

I am a great listener

Listening is the key to great communication with your child. It is the basis of a strong relationship. If you listen to them when they are young, they will be much more inclined to want you to listen to them as they grow older and face the challenges of their teenage years. Children are the greatest talkers and every mum gets a lot of practice. This chapter is about developing your skill of listening at a deeper level. It is about really hearing what it is your child has to say. And it is also about talking so that your child will want to listen to what you have to say.

▶ Your child will feel **valued and secure**

▶ Your child will feel able to **talk openly to you** about their feelings and their worries

▶ You will help your child to develop **valuable listening skills**

mum as coach

As a mum, you have many roles and responsibilities in your child's life. When they are small, they are totally dependent on you. Then they grow older and begin to develop their own friendships and interests. You become the logistical expert and taxi driver, managing their social diaries, play dates and clubs. Throughout your child's life, one of your most significant roles will be as their coach. It is an exciting role, helping your child make the transition from being dependent to being independent.

As your child's coach, you will demonstrate many skills as you support them on their journey through life. You are not behind or in front – you are with them every step of the way. You are helping your child to identify what they want to do, setting exciting and achievable targets – and giving them the confidence and motivation to achieve their goals. You empower your child to take responsibility for their lives – and to enjoy that responsibility.

The more successful you are as a coach, the greater their happiness, confidence and self-belief will be.

the signs of a great coach

Great coaches have the ability to listen, to ask excellent questions, to focus on solutions, to boost confidence and to motivate.

As a mum, you will already have these skills in abundance. You have been learning them since the day your child was born. The most important skill is listening because, without this, none of the others are possible.

I am listening – or am I?

Every mum knows just how often she says 'I'm listening' – usually to several children and several conversations at once! Your child is desperate for your attention and you do your best to please everyone – without actually being able to hear a thing. You want to please everyone but you can end up pleasing no one. Not only that, you can feel as though your life has no volume control – and your head is going stir crazy. There is too much noise for you to think, let alone think straight. Listening as a mum is very difficult. Accept that it is a real challenge. You know how good you feel when someone is really paying you attention and listening to you. You also know how bad you feel when someone says they are listening to you – and you know they are not. It is the same for your child. They are experts. They know exactly when you are listening and exactly when you are not.

listen 100 per cent some of the time

The truth of the matter is that you can't listen properly to everything that your child wants to tell you. Don't feel guilty about it. You are not superwoman, so stop trying to do the impossible.

What you can do is develop your listening skills so that, when you do listen, you are **really** listening. It is better to spend 5 minutes really listening and hearing what they have to say than to spend 50 minutes not really listening.

By developing your own skills, you will also be helping your child develop valuable skills. You will be sending them a powerful message about the importance of listening and they will learn to listen to you and everyone else around them in a different way.

instant listening boosters

▶ **stop**
▶ **Saying 'I'm listening' when you aren't**
▶ **Trying to listen over the TV**
▶ **Talking more than you listen**

▶ **start**
▶ **Saying 'I'm listening' when you are**
▶ **Getting down to your children's level when you are listening**
▶ **Listening with your eyes as well as your ears. Look at them and it will boost their confidence**

learn to be a good listener

A survey by the Parent Coaching Academy reveals that, although most mums often say they are listening, they are not hearing what their children have to say. Think what happens in your own home. Imagine how different your family life would be if you did less talking and more real listening.

1 are you really listening?

Be honest and say when you are listening and when you are not listening. If you are not in a position to listen to your child, tell them. Say what you mean and mean what you say. You may think that, by saying you are listening, you are trying to be positive with them and letting them know you care – but they will know when you are not being honest.

Let you child know that you are only human and that you are trying to listen to them better because you really love hearing what they have to say. Your child will get the message that you care much more powerfully if you are honest.

walk and talk

Walking with your child provides more opportunity to listen to them than travelling in the car, when you have other things on your mind. Walk with them as often as you can – and enjoy each journey.

facts about listening
- 9 out of 10 mums say they frequently say they are listening when they are not
- 9 out of 10 mums say they find trying to listen to more than one child at once 'very stressful'
- 8 out of 10 mums say they do more talking than listening

2 the listening quiz

Take a look at the ten skills listed below and for each of them decide whether you are: A – Strong; B – OK; C – Weak.

Listening skill	A	B	C
I listen to my child and hear what they have to say	☐	☐	☐
I encourage my child to talk when there is a gap in conversation – not over other people	☐	☐	☐
I listen more often than I talk	☐	☐	☐
I listen with my eyes as well as my ears	☐	☐	☐
I encourage my child to be in the same room as me when they want me to listen	☐	☐	☐
I praise my child when they listen to me well	☐	☐	☐
I praise my child when they listen to their friends and other people	☐	☐	☐
I enjoy at least 10 minutes quality 'listening' time at least once a day	☐	☐	☐
I can tune in to my child and understand what makes them tick	☐	☐	☐
I only say I am listening when I really mean it	☐	☐	☐
Total out of 10	☐	☐	☐

how did you score?

Mostly As You have well-developed skills and are a great role model.
Mostly Bs You are doing well. You have a good foundation to build on.
Mostly Cs You are being honest with yourself. That is vital if you want to move forwards. Make changes and you will see quick improvements.

who talks most?

It may not always seem like it, but in most homes, it is the mums – not the children – who do most of the talking. Over the next day, rise to the challenge of listening to your child more than talking to them and you will be surprised at just how much you find out about them.

3 the 10-minute listening challenge

Create 10 minutes to actively tune in to your child today – just as you would to a radio station. Make sure you are receiving their signals loud and clear and that there is no interference.

involve your child

▶ Tell them what you love about hearing them talk

▶ Give positive and specific feedback

▶ Enjoy learning something new about each child

By doing this, you will show them that you really are listening and hearing what they have to say. Every time you set a good listening example, you are helping your child to be a good listener too.

Always listen more than you talk. Remember that you have two ears and one mouth for a very good reason.

ask good questions

As well as developing effective listening skills, it is essential that you know what questions to ask and the best way to ask them. As a mum, the better the questions you ask, the better their responses will be and the more you will be able to really tune in to what they are saying and how they are feeling about themselves and life.

follow the flow
Don't have a set agenda when it comes to asking questions – go where your child leads you. Listen to what they say and ask a question relating to what they have said. It will show that you are listening and take your conversation to a deeper level.

1 ask the right type of question

There are two different types of questions – **closed** questions and **open** questions. The table below shows the differences between them.

Closed questions	Open questions
Often start with 'Do' or 'Are'	Often start with 'How' or 'What'
Often prompt a one-word answer – usually 'Yes' or 'No'	Often prompt a more creative and descriptive answer
Close doors and limit conversation	Open doors and encourage conversation
Don't give your child the opportunity to express their thoughts and feelings	Give your child a good opportunity to express their thoughts and feelings
Reduce the quality of communication between you and your child	Improve the quality of communication between you and your child

Here are some examples of closed and open questions:

Closed	Open
Did you enjoy school?	What did you do that was fun at school today?
What football team do you support?	What do you enjoy most about watching your favourite football team?
What book are you reading at the moment?	Imagine you are Harry Potter. Can you tell me what you are like?

your question rating
Think about the questions that you ask. Which type of questions do you ask more: closed questions or open questions? How good are you at asking open questions? Most people don't do it naturally. It takes practice.

   Give yourself a rating on a scale of 1 to 10 – where 10 means that you are great at open questions and 1 indicates plenty of room for improvement.

2 the 24-hour question challenge

Focus today on asking more open questions. Before you speak, think about the words you want to use. You will probably find you have to make a conscious effort to do this. You may be breaking the habits of a lifetime, but the more you get into the habit of asking open questions, the easier it will become. Persist – even when your toddler or teenager is grunting back. We all know that this can be a one-way street – but keep at it and you will see the results. By making positive changes in **your communication skills** you will eventually bring about positive changes in **your child's skills** as well.

3 dump the 'why' word

Questions beginning with 'Why' tend to make us and our children feel negative and defensive. Think about how you feel when people ask you a question beginning with 'Why?' What words would you use to describe the way you feel? It is likely that your child feels the same way.

Your challenge is to **see how far you can get through today without using the word 'Why'.**

make the most of mealtimes

Family mealtimes are a fantastic opportunity for you to listen to your child talk. When you are eating, cut out any interference. Switch the TV off and your answer machine on. Make sure your child knows this is a special time for all of you.

involve your child

Your child learns everything from you, especially when it comes to communication. By boosting your listening and questioning skills, you are having a direct impact on one of the most important areas of their life.

1 play Ear-Spy

We all know how to play I-Spy, so now **try Ear-Spy**. It is fun and encourages everyone to listen. Choose a sound that you want your child to listen for – laughter, traffic, wind, aeroplane, dog barking – and see how quickly they can hear it. Or get them to listen for certain words, for example, whenever you say 'it', 'and' or 'but'. See how many times they can catch you saying the word in 5 minutes.

lower your voice

Lower the volume of your own voice. This will encourage your child to listen more effectively.

2 praise your child for listening well

The best way to reinforce good listening habits in your child is to give them specific positive praise when they listen well. As mums we are much more likely to praise our children for what they say rather than for their listening skills, but both are equally important.

Look at the listening wheel below. It gives some examples of the listening skills you can praise your child for. **Focus on one skill each day.** You can use stickers or stars if you think that will help to motivate them.

This is a great way for you to talk to your child about listening and the importance of giving people the time and space to talk. They can help you set some listening rules for your family and add their own ideas to the wheel to help you all.

turn off the TV
Children often watch quite a bit of TV, but encourage them to listen to the radio too and stories on CD and tape. It will help them to focus on listening and understanding without visual cues.

YOUR CHILD'S IDEAS

Be in the same room when talking to each other

Play Ear-Spy

Stop what you are doing to listen

Listen to a story tape together

Look at the person who is talking

Listen as you read a story and tell you about it

Take it in turns to talk

3 play the listening game

Place two chairs back to back – one for you and one for your child – so that you are facing in opposite directions. You each have a piece of paper. Ask your child to draw a simple picture on her paper and, as she draws it, to describe it to you. Your aim is to listen to everything she says and to try to replicate the picture on your piece of paper. When she has finished, take a look and see how close you are.

Now it is your turn to draw a picture and describe it to your child. This activity is great fun and it will really help you to focus on your listening and communication skills.

I am fun and not frantic

As a mum, you have absolutely no idea where all your time goes. There is always so much to do and never enough time to do it. You used to think you were organized. But the days seem to fly by and you can't get nearly to the bottom of your 'to do' list. You know that, no matter how hard you try to squeeze everything in, there will never be enough hours in the day. Before you had a child, you were looking forward to being a fun mum. But now you have them, it is a different story – and you have become a frantic mum instead.

▶ If you are a frantic mum, your child is more likely to be **frantic** too

▶ Fun mums have **fun families** and create **happy memories** for their child

▶ Happy families are **healthy** families. The more you laugh, the longer you are likely to live

family rush hours

All mums know that, if they had a time machine, family life would be easy. They would simply be able to whizz backwards and forwards in time fitting 3 hours' worth of work into 10 minutes. But they don't.

A survey by the Parent Coaching Academy revealed that 8 out of 10 mums say they would **often** describe themselves as 'frantic' during the course of a normal family day. They say that mornings are the most stressful time, with evenings a close second. Many mums also say that they also find weekends frantic and stressful rather than being calm and relaxing.

the quality time pressure cooker

There are always so many pressures on your time as a mum. There are hundreds of things for you to think about and get sorted – and that is just before breakfast! As a parent, you have to be a logistical expert. Just getting out of the house in the morning – making sure your child is dressed, has had breakfast, cleaned their teeth and have their schoolbag – is a major achievement. On a good day, they may even get matching socks.

But that isn't all. Every time you open a newspaper, watch TV or listen to the radio, there seems to be a story telling you what you **should** or **shouldn't** be doing with your time, and about the importance of spending quality time with your son or daughter. This places even more pressure on you as a mum. You are not only expected to be superhuman and fit everything in but you are also expected to find quality time with your family.

mums are the best time managers

As a mum, you can consider yourself to be the managing director of the most important company in the world – your family. There is a good reason why you struggle to get everything done. It is because being a mum and running a family is a major challenge. It is also one of the toughest, most demanding and stressful jobs you will ever do.

According to 9 out of 10 employers, mums are not only excellent time managers but also have the following skills:

- ▶ They are focused
- ▶ They use their time creatively
- ▶ They are multi-skilled and flexible
- ▶ They are productive
- ▶ They are able to work under pressure in order to meet deadlines

You may give yourself a hard time because you want to do it all, but look at the evidence and you will see that actually you have great strengths when it comes to managing your time. You just don't appreciate the size of your challenge and all you achieve on a daily basis.

fun mums have fun families

Believe that you can take control of your time rather than letting time take control of you. If you believe that you don't have enough time, you will be proved absolutely right. If you believe that you can find time to do what you want, you will.

Do you want your child to grow up in a frantic world where everyone is rushing around and trying to pack as much in as possible – even if it means high stress levels? Do you want them to live in a world where life is just one long deadline?

Or do you want your child to live in a fun world, with time to smell the flowers and enjoy the precious moments of their childhood. Do you want your child to live for the moment and have the time to appreciate what being in a loving family is all about? Do you want a fun family or a frantic family? The decision is yours.

instant 'fun mum' boosters

▷ **stop**

▷ **Trying to pack as much as possible into every day**

▷ **Worrying about everything you have to do**

▷ **Thinking 'lack of time'**

▷ **Frowning**

▷ **start**

▷ **Doing less and enjoying it more**

▷ **Do one thing that is fun before 9.00 am every day**

▷ **Thinking 'lots of' time**

▷ **Smiling**

take control of your time

You may not have a time machine, but you can still be a master of your time instead of being a time slave – if you believe you can. You already make many important and good decisions about how you and your family spend their time. It is time to take your game to the next level.

1 be positive about time

Today is the moment to get back into the driving seat. Instead of letting life run away with you, think positive and start creating the life that you want. **Commit to take control of your time** – and enjoy it! If you are positive about time, your family will be too. Today, instead of talking about what you haven't done or don't have time to do, start talking about what you have achieved with your time and what you enjoyed doing with it.

invest your time

Instead of wasting time worrying about all there is to do, invest your time in creating a positive frame of mind that will help you to use the time you do have more effectively.

2 the fun or frantic quiz

When it comes to time, mums are experts at being self-critical. But instead of focusing on what you don't get done, it is time to celebrate the skills and qualities you already have that help you to achieve a huge amount every minute of every day. Appreciating your strengths will help you feel better equipped to deal with the daily time challenges that family life throws at you.

Look at the fun qualities in the table below and decide how you would describe yourself for each of them: A – Strong; B – OK.

Fun quality	A	B
I can get in touch with the child within me		
I smile more often than I frown		
I am good at prioritizing what I want to do with my time		
I encourage my child to prioritize their time		
I control my housework – it doesn't control me		
I have fun with my child every day		
I work effectively under pressure to meet deadlines		
I value the precious time I have with my family		
I am good at delegating		
I set myself realistic goals to achieve		

how did you score?
Mostly As You are a fun mum and a strong time manager. You rise to the time challenges of daily family life.
Mostly Bs You are doing OK but life is a bit more frantic than fun. You would notice the difference if you made some small changes.

create 10 minutes of 'me' time

Invest in a giant egg timer, it'll be a great prop for you. Use it to enjoy 10 minutes of 'me' time when you stop running round and sit down to relax. Get into the habit of doing it every day.

3 the 24-hour time creation challenge

Take another look at the statements in the table and your responses to them. **Choose one area that you would like to focus on over the next 24 hours.** It may be an area where you feel there is definite room for improvement. Or it may be an area where you are already good but want to be even better.

Write out the statement exactly as it appears in the table and put it somewhere very visible. Then make it happen – at least once – today.

be positive about time creation

You are like most mums. From the moment your alarm goes off, the clock is like a time bomb ticking in your head. You are rushing from one deadline to the next and are in danger of missing them all.

1 stop the 'no time' battle cries

'You are making us late!'. 'There isn't time!'. 'You will have to do that later!'. 'Hurry up!'. These are your desperate daily battle cries. You are usually raising your voice or shouting and you can feel the signs of physical tension.

However, the more you repeat these cries, the more stressed you and your child will feel. You may think it helps to say the same thing over and over again, but it doesn't. It just puts all of you under more pressure and makes you **less likely** – not **more likely** – to meet your deadline.

See what a difference it can make if you stop your battle cries for just one day?

give your battle cry the red card
Identify one specific time-related battle cry you use and see how far you can get through the day without using it.
Rather than telling your child what there isn't time to do, **explain what you do want them to do in the time available.**
Make sure that the time frame you are setting for your child to achieve a task is realistic. Something that takes you 5 minutes may take a child a lot longer.

By focusing on what you say, you are taking an important step away from being a frantic mum. You are making a conscious effort to make changes and this will help you to stop raising your voice and feel calmer. You and your child will always achieve more when you are feeling less stressed.

2 life is about choices

Life is about choices. You are constantly making decisions about what to do with your time – and you are much more likely to find the time to do something you **want** to do rather than something you feel you **ought** to do.

Look at the activities below. If you wanted to reduce **one** activity by 10 minutes today – so that you could spend an extra 10 minutes being a fun mum – from **where would you take the time?** It needs to be within your control because then **you can make it happen**.

- ☐ Sleeping
- ☐ Working
- ☐ On the phone
- ☐ Housework
- ☐ Chores outside the home, such as shopping
- ☐ Watching TV/working on the computer
- ☐ Child's activities, such as clubs, play dates
- ☐ Other

Once you have made your decision, **make it happen**.

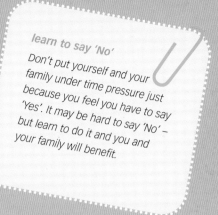

learn to say 'No'

Don't put yourself and your family under time pressure just because you feel you have to say 'Yes'. It may be hard to say 'No' – but learn to do it and you and your family will benefit.

3 do, delegate or ditch

Recognize that you can't do everything, so try the 'do, delegate or ditch' approach for a day:

▶ **Do** only what you really want to get done

▶ **Delegate** as much as you can

▶ **Ditch** the rest

It is impossible to get to the end of a 'to do' list if you are constantly adding to it. By prioritizing your time and setting yourself achievable goals, you will be much more productive.

treat time as a challenge not a threat

Children respond well to challenges. You will be surprised just how quickly they can get dressed or find their schoolbag if you challenge them to do it against the clock. Use your giant egg-timer and watch them go.

skill builder
make time

What better incentive can you have for leaving work on time, leaving the laundry in the basket or switching off your mobile phone, than to enjoy precious time with your child? The activities below suggest some ways of making time and using it creatively.

1 the 10-minute time creation challenge

Take a look at the time creation wheel below. You probably have plenty of great ideas of your own. Here are some more to help you create more time to spend with your family – and to be a fun mum not a frantic one.

Each idea will provide you with at least an extra 10 minutes of fun mum time.

Time creation wheel:
- YOUR IDEA
- Set your alarm clock for 10 minutes earlier
- Leave work on time
- Set a time limit for the housework
- Draw up a family roster for sharing chores
- Buy your shopping on-line
- Switch on your answering machine
- Switch off your mobile phone

Choose one of the ideas that you want to put into action.

don't
Focus on all of the reasons why you can't make it happen.

do
Focus on all of the reasons why you do want to make it happen.

2 make a fantasy fun list

Now the real fun begins. If you are really committed to creating the time to enjoy being a mum, you will succeed.

Spend time with your child brainstorming a list of fun activities you would like to do together. Think blue sky and all the things you could do together – not just the things that you have already done.

make it visible
Write your fun list on a large piece of paper and put it somewhere very visible. You and your child can add to it at any time.

make it happen
Decide what activity you are going to do together this week and put it in your diary. We often use a diary to make sure we don't forget dental appointments and birthdays, but we rarely put a date with our children into the diary. The more specific you are about the time you are going to do this, the more likely it is to happen. For example, instead of saying 'over the weekend', commit yourself to 2.30 pm on Saturday and it is much more likely to happen.

If you have more than one child, it is good to make a list that includes special one-to-one mum time for each of them. Of course you have to be organized to make it happen – and you will be if you really want to.

get out and about

Nine out of ten mums say that they find it much easier to be a fun mum when they are out of the home and not distracted by housework.

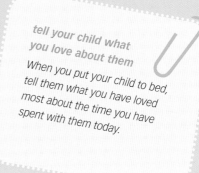

tell your child what you love about them

When you put your child to bed, tell them what you have loved most about the time you have spent with them today.

3 press the pause button at mealtimes

Make mealtimes a priority. The frantic pace of life means mealtimes are often rushed and many families rarely sit down and eat together. However, they are one of the most important times in a family's day. Take your time and enjoy each other's company. It may not be possible for you all to sit down for a meal every day because of work and other commitments – but aim to do it **at least once a week**. Make it **a regular family event** that you all value and look forward to.

troubleshooting

You gave up work to be a full-time mum, but you don't seem to spending much time with your children. There is always too much housework to do. The days fly by and you feel guilty about not spending enough time playing with them.

▶ Many mums feel exactly the same. They want to spend time with their children but end up spending more time with the vacuum cleaner.

▶ Stop putting yourself under pressure to have the perfect family **house** – family **homes** are much more fun. What makes a home special are the experiences

that your family share together – not tidy toy boxes. Keep reminding yourself that the housework will always be there, but the children won't be small for long. Fit housework around the children, not the other way around. Or get them involved in the housework!

▶ Set yourself realistic housework targets. There will always be something that needs doing, but decide between how long you want to spend on jobs and how much you could really achieve in that time. It will help you to prioritize your tasks and be more productive. Put time in your diary for tasks and outings.

▶ Get out of the house at least once a day with the children. Getting out and about, even for a 10-minute walk, will blow away the cobwebs and give you precious time together. The housework won't seem so important when you get back.

You are starting to dread your days off work because they are so stressful. You want to have fun, but your toddler's tantrums are making your life a misery. You end up shouting and feeling guilty because you are not really enjoying the time that you and your son have together.

▷ Toddler tantrums increase stress levels and many mums end up shouting. There is also extra pressure on you because it is your day off and you want to enjoy the limited time you have with your toddler.

▷ A positive frame of mind is the key to success. If you are feeling negative about your day off, both you and your toddler will be tense. Take a few minutes to focus on what you love most about your toddler and what you treasure about spending precious time together.

▷ Act your age not your child's. If you stamp your feet to get what you want – that is what he will do, too. But you can change his behaviour by setting a good example. Catch him red-handed being good but ignore his bad behaviour. At the moment, you are giving him lots of attention. It may be shouting and a telling-off, but it is still attention. Only give him attention for the behaviour that you want to encourage.

▷ Give your day off a fun focus. Decide on one specific activity you want to enjoy together – and do it.

You really look forward to weekends and holidays. You like to spend family days out, but you always find the trips really stressful instead of enjoyable.

▷ Family fun days are really important but they do take energy and organizing and can be stressful.

▷ Make the journey as stress-free as possible. Declutter the car and you will set off in a positive frame of mind. Take snacks and drinks, and things to amuse the children on the journey, and think up games, such as I-Spy.

▷ See the day through your children's eyes instead of yours and you will enjoy it much more. Think of excitement – not endurance. Aim for connection – not perfection. Have a giggle – not a grumble.

▷ Don't rush around trying to pack in as many activities as you can. Slow down and enjoy doing what you **want** to do. Don't ignore signs of boredom, tiredness or hunger in your children. Look out for the tell-tale signs and act on them before they develop into a full-blown tantrum – yours or your child's.

▷ Involve your children in setting a good behaviour goal for the day. Praise their good behaviour (stickers work a treat on a day out) – and let them set a behaviour goal for you too.

▷ Build in regular physical activity – for you and the family – throughout the day. This releases tension, burns up energy and will help you all feel less stressed.

I am a stress manager

Most mums agree that the pressures of day-to-day family life can seem overwhelming at times. You may think that stress is something you can't control. It is true that there may be factors outside of your control that cause you stress, However, the way that you respond to these factors **is** within your control and, because you are in control, **you** can reduce your stress levels. Developing a positive attitude to stress is important, not just for you, but for your child and the rest of your family. The way you handle pressure will also have a direct impact on your child and their ability to handle stress.

►You will be **happier and healthier**, with more **energy** to enjoy your family

►High stress levels stop you and your child **achieving your potential**

►By handling your own stress well, you will help your child to develop their own **strategies for handling stress**

feeling more stressed now you are a mum is normal

You may have thought that you handled stress well until you had a family. You may have been used to the responsibility of a stressful job and working under pressure.

However, now you have a child, your stress stakes have jumped right up the scale. You may have noticed that, since becoming a mum, you seem to worry much more than you did before. Many mums say that, as well as worrying about major issues, such as health, childcare and education, they find themselves feeling stressed about many smaller things that they once took in their stride. You may find that normal everyday activities – booking the child in for a dentist's appointment, organizing a babysitter, sorting out a packed lunch or finding time to help with homework – can seem overwhelming at times.

recognizing stress

A certain amount of stress in our lives is natural – and being a mum is one of the toughest challenges you will ever face. Every day presents new problems to solve. Life can be particularly stressful if you are struggling to combine family life with a career.

Up to a point, your increased stress levels are normal. Having children brings a huge increase in responsibility. You are not just responsible for yourself anymore. You have a child who is dependent on you and who will be around for a lifetime. It is an awesome responsibility and you put yourself under pressure because you want to get it right.

However, be careful not to let your stress levels get too high. Watch out for the warning signs – when you start to find life totally overwhelming and out of your control, and you feel unable to cope. As a result you say things to your children that you would never say if your were more relaxed and you stop being the mum you want to be.

real mums beat supermums

One of the reasons you feel under so much stress is because you want to be all things to all people. Mums are great at looking after everyone else but not so good at looking after themselves. You are a real mum in the real world – not a supermum – and that is the most fantastic place to be. Being a real mum, instead of trying to be a supermum, will mean a happier and healthier family.

teach your child to handle stress well

The way you embrace life's challenges will have a direct impact on the way your child grows up and the way they learn to deal with problems in life. Once you start focusing positively on the way you respond to difficult situations, your child will learn to do the same. It used to be the case that children were just that – young, carefree, vibrant and stress-free. Today, however, children's experiences can be quite different. There can be a lot more pressure on them and they are exposed to a whole range of situations that can increase their stress levels – at home, at play and at school.

A childhood that is as stress-free as possible is a great goal for any mum to aim for. And the starting point is you.

real mums beat supermums

▶ **supermums**

▶ **Never admit that they are struggling**

▶ **Have perfect houses**

▶ **Exist**

▶ **Set unrealistic targets for themselves and their children**

▶ **Are predictable and boring**

▶ **real mums**

▶ **Are honest and know family life can be tough**

▶ **Have family homes**

▶ **Live life to the full**

▶ **Set realistic targets for themselves and their children**

▶ **Are fun and unpredictable**

assess your stress levels

*You may have a lot of challenges in your life that are affecting your stress levels. You may be experiencing stressful situations at work or at home that are particularly tough. Your life may bring you into contact with some difficult and negative people. Many of these things may be out of your control. But you **can control** the way in which you respond to them.*

1 your stress rating

Take a look at the list below and decide how many of the ten tell-tale signs of a stressed mum apply to you.

- [ ] You deal in fears not fact
- [ ] You are negative
- [ ] You believe your life is out of control
- [ ] You see problems everywhere
- [ ] You talk about solving problems but do nothing
- [ ] You are paralysed with fear
- [ ] You are a can't-do mum
- [ ] You exist rather than living life to the full
- [ ] You are isolated
- [ ] You avoid challenges

Give yourself a stress rating out of 10. Imagine how you would feel if you could reduce your stress rating to 0. What will be the greatest benefit to you of being able to reduce your stress levels? How will it benefit your family?

take responsibility

You can't control other people and what they do, but you can take responsibility for **yourself** and what **you** do. The more you feel your life is out of control, the greater your stress levels. By taking control, you will reduce your stress levels.

2

the stress-handling quiz

Many of the things that you do already can help you to handle the challenges in your life. As a mum, you often cope brilliantly with stressful situations. It is important that you recognize what you do well – and encourage your child to do the same.

Take a look at the statements in the table below and tick your answers: 'Yes' or 'No'.

Stress-handling skill	Yes	No
I can deal in facts	☐	☐
I can be positive	☐	☐
I can feel in control of my life	☐	☐
I can see solutions not problems	☐	☐
I can take action to solve problems	☐	☐
I can feel relaxed	☐	☐
I can move forward with purpose instead of being paralysed with fear	☐	☐
I can get support	☐	☐
I can embrace challenges	☐	☐
I am a can-do mum	☐	☐

how did you score?
Mostly 'Yes' You embrace challenges and have low stress levels. You have confidence and believe in yourself.
Mostly 'No' You avoid challenges and have high stress levels. You don't believe in your ability to handle stress well. Only you can change this.

---

the 'I can' challenge

As a mum, you are a great creative problem-solver. You do it all the time. Believe in yourself and your ability to handle stressful situations well. Today, when you are feeling stressed about one of life's challenges, say to yourself, **'I can do this'** – and you will. And if **you** do this, your child will learn to do it too.

3

the 'I can' challenge

Mums with a positive frame of mind handle challenges more effectively and have lower levels of stress. The more time you spend thinking about how stressed you are, the more stressed you will feel. It is better to invest your time in helping yourself to feel as positive as possible.

focus on the things you do well and avoid stress by
▶ breaking big tasks into small components

▶ prioritizing the tasks that need to be done

▶ allocating a set time for each task

▶ giving yourself a treat for completing a task

Believe that you **do** have strengths and skills and qualities to help you handle pressure.

spring-clean your family life

One of the factors that increases stress in family life is clutter – emotional and physical. It gets in the way and drains your energy. If you want to be in the best frame of mind to deal with the pressures of family life, you want clarity and order – in your mind and in your home.

1 declutter your mind

Get into the habit of clearing your mind of negative thoughts in the same way as you clear out your wardrobe. Negative thoughts drain your energy and make you feel less able to cope. When you are up against life's challenges, it is often easier to fill your mind with powerful negative thoughts.

Get rid of these negative thoughts. Close your eyes and count to 30. As you count, take a deep breath and focus on your breathing. Feel the breath fill your body and mind with energy, sweeping out the old negative thoughts and making room for new positive thoughts.

Fill the space with a vibrant picture of your child. See every detail of their face as they smile at you. Look deep into their eyes and feel the connection. Your relationship is what is important in life.

relaxation
Learn how to relax. If you want to cope with challenges, you have to look after yourself. Learn a new relaxation technique that you can put into practice on a daily basis, such as yoga or meditation.

2 declutter your house

By decluttering your house, your garden and your car, you can make a real difference to your state of mind – not just to your family home.

Look at the clutter wheel below and decide which area you would most like to declutter. You may find it helpful to go into a room, sit in your car or pick up your handbag and decide which of them brings out the most stressful feelings in you.

YOUR IDEA

Kitchen

Car

TV room

Handbag or baby rucksack

Your child's room

Your bedroom

Bathroom

don't procrastinate

If you are facing a problem that is causing you stress, commit yourself to tackling it. Putting it off will only increase your stress levels. By dealing with it, no matter how difficult it may be, you will reduce your stress levels.

3 the 10-minute declutter challenge

Arm yourself with a bin liner or carrier bag and give yourself 10-minutes to declutter a specific stress area – perhaps an area that you have identified from the clutter wheel or another that is relevant to you. It is your choice.

As you clear the clutter in your home, you will feel a weight lifting from your shoulders and a new clarity of mind – as well as having much more space. It feels great. As you declutter, you will reduce your stress levels and increase your energy levels.

Take any items that you are recycling to an organization that will appreciate them – such as a charity, school or nursery, or a family you know who could really use them. **Do this today if possible.**

room for improvement

Once you have got rid of all the junk, stand in the middle of the room, sit in the car or hold your handbag and take a good look round. Enjoy the moment. Now think of one positive practical thing that you can do to make the room, the car or your handbag even better – this will also make a real difference to your state of mind.

For example, you could:

▶ Spring-clean
▶ Rearrange the furniture
▶ Paint a wall a different colour
▶ Buy a new lamp
▶ Buy a plant
▶ Put up a picture
▶ Label the toy boxes
▶ Get your car cleaned

learn to handle stress

In today's busy and demanding world, it is not only mums who feel stressed – children feel stress as well. Even little ones can feel that life is full of pressure and deadlines. If you handle stress well, your children will learn to do so too.

1 count your blessings and get problems in perspective

Focus on your child and your special relationship with them. This will help you get your everyday problems into perspective. Cuddle your child. Take a good look at them and feel the connection between you. Recognize that, while life may be challenging, you have so much to be thankful for. You are a mum and that is special.

get in touch with the child within you

Children know how to relax and have fun – and that is what all mums need to do. Play will reduce your stress levels – but only if you aren't looking at your watch and thinking about what you have to do next. Forget the dishwasher, the laundry and the shopping and live and laugh in the moment.

2 identify your priorities

If you keep doing what you are doing in the same way, you will keep on getting what you are getting. If you want to feel less stressed you have **to do something differently**. Instead of standing still and feeling paralysed, you can take action and move forward one step at a time.

Don't try to deal with everything at once. It can be too much and you may end up doing nothing at all. Break down the big picture and identify one specific area that you can work on and do things that are within your control. Focus on where you want to go – and head there.

Look at the problem wheel below. It shows some of the problems that many mums are faced with. **Create your own problem wheel and write down the problems that are causing you stress at the moment and that you want to do something about.** The examples will give you some ideas.

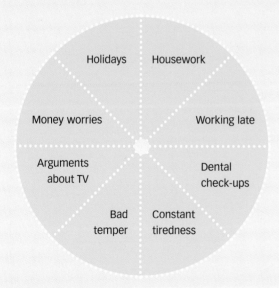

Holidays

Housework

Money worries

Working late

Arguments about TV

Dental check-ups

Bad temper

Constant tiredness

Decide which one problem you want to make your priority in the next 24 hours. It may be the most stressful or it may be one that is easiest to cross off your list.

3 find a solution

Instead of thinking about the problem, **focus on what the solution might be.** What do you want to be happening? How do you want to feel? What do you want to be saying?

Brainstorm all the things you can do that are within your control. This will help to take you one step closer to the solution you have identified. Choose **one thing** and **do** it. Take the first step. The first step is always the most important. It means you are committing yourself to take action about the problem. The table below gives some examples.

Problem	First step to a solution
The house is a mess	Ask your partner to look after the children for 2 hours on Saturday so you can get it under control – or book a cleaner for a one-off spring-clean
It is hard to leave work on time	Arrange a meeting with your manager to talk about solutions to your workload
The children keep arguing about the TV	Draw up a schedule of times they can watch and whose turn it is to choose the channel
I am worried about money and spending too much	Phone your bank and ask for a list of all standing orders and direct debits. List all your outgoings and see where cuts can be made

get support – together you are stronger

You are not alone. Once you have identified what you can do to help yourself deal with a stressful situation, identify specific support that would help to reduce your stress levels – and get it **today**. It can come from any of a number of places, such as family, friends, health or education professionals, your line manager or a charity.

troubleshooting

Being a parent is much more tiring and stressful than you and your partner imagined. You seem to be constantly nagging him to help you around the house and having big row over little things, such as who loads the dishwasher or who cooks the dinner.

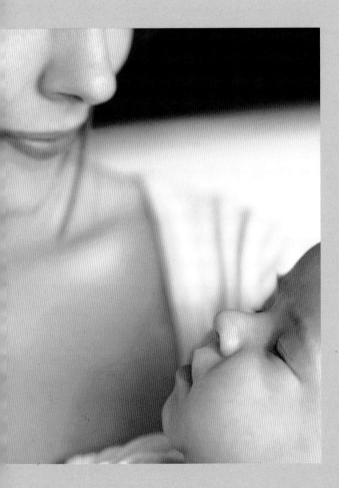

▶ You are both learning to adapt. You now have a child who is totally dependent on you, so your relationship is bound to change.

▶ When you are tired, it can be easy to find fault with your partner. Commit today to telling him what he has done well rather than what he hasn't done – and there will be lots of things. When he is at his most irritating, look at him and see the man you love – not the man who can't stack the dishwasher properly.

▶ Your partner is different from you. You are a skilled logistical expert, but he probably sees your organization as nagging – a never-ending 'to do' list. Instead of telling him what to do, ask him to suggest ways in which you can support each other. Try to tune in to your partner and to see family life through his eyes. You will understand him better.

▶ Good relationships don't just happen – they need work. Give your partner a cuddle and tell him you love him. Or surprise him and book a babysitter so that you can have a night out together.

When you had your child, you decided that you wanted to be around for them and only work part-time. Now you feel really stressed because money is tight and you are wondering how you are going to manage and whether you have made the right decision.

▶ The question about going back to work – either full-time, part-time or not at all – is a big decision for all mums. Every mum has a great gut instinct and you will have made the decision that is right for you. Instead of finding reasons to worry, find ways to make it work.

▶ Financial pressures are very stressful, usually because mums feel they are outside their control. Commit yourself, today, to take control of your family finances instead of letting them control you.

▶ Your resources may be limited, but what you do with them is up to you. Work out exactly what your income is and make a list of all your essential outgoings. Explore all childcare possibilities for the days when you are working and include it in your budget.

▶ Draw out the amount of money that you can afford to spend each week and pay by cash instead of by credit card. This will make you very aware of where the money goes.

▶ Set yourself a challenge. For example, if you want to save £25 a week, how would you do it?

▶ Finally, remember that money is only money while being a mum is priceless. You may have less cash, but you will have experiences to treasure forever.

Your baby is gorgeous, but you find being a mum is much more stressful than you ever imagined. You are permanently shattered and there is always so much to do. For much of the time you feel very stressed – especially when your baby cries.

▶ Your feelings are natural. You are coming to terms with a life-changing experience. No one can prepare you for this – and babies don't come with an instruction booklet.

▶ Anyone who uses the phrase 'sleeping like a baby' has obviously never had one. Looking after a baby is hard work, and you are on call for 24 hours, 7 days of the week. New mums get very tired. The exhaustion that comes from broken nights can cause havoc and makes even simple tasks seem impossible.

▶ Don't use baby's sleep time to catch up on all the jobs that need doing around the house. Have a sleep yourself – or treat yourself to a bath or read a magazine.

▶ Listening to your baby cry is stressful. Decide whether you want to get some support to help you cope with the crying. If you do, make an appointment to talk to your doctor or health visitor. Take a note of when your baby usually cries, and for how long, and of any specific patterns that you notice. Take a list of the questions that you would like answered – this is easier than trying to remember them on the spot.

I am a confidence booster

You are a mum, so you will know just how much you want your children to believe in themselves. You are the person who can have the most powerful positive impact on their confidence. They will carry what they learn to believe about themselves when they are small throughout their lives. You know how important confidence is in your own life. If you think you can – you will. If you think you can't – you will be proved absolutely right. The same is true of your child. Given confidence, everything is possible.

2

the three-step 'I can' plan

You can help them by taking positive and practical action whenever you hear your children saying something negative about themselves:

▶ **Challenge their negative language.** Give them specific examples of skills they have that will help them to do what they want to do. Give them evidence to feel positive about themselves.

▶ **Break down the task.** Help them to identify small, specific steps they **can** achieve.

▶ **Praise them.** When they achieve each step, praise them. As each step is completed, encourage them to say, **'I can'**.

By challenging their negative self-beliefs, giving positive evidence to demonstrate your reason for this and helping them develop an achievable action plan, you will have a direct impact on your child's confidence and self-belief.

stop making personal remarks

Most mums make personal remarks about their children at one time or another, especially in the heat of the moment. But the limiting beliefs we have about ourselves as adults often develop as a result of a remark made to us by a person in authority – such as a parent or teacher – when we were young. If you want to make a point to your child, make it clear that it is about their behaviour and not about them personally.

all-round confidence

As parents, we are sometimes tempted to focus our attention on the areas in which our children feel least confident. However, boosting their confidence in an area that they feel good about will help boost their self-belief generally and give them greater confidence to tackle the subjects and life issues that they find a struggle.

3

go on a feeling-finding mission

By helping your child to talk openly and honestly about their feelings – both positive and negative – you are helping to build their confidence.

negative feelings
It is important to **acknowledge your child's negative feelings and put yourself in their shoes.** As mums, we sometimes want to respond to 'I'm worried' with 'Don't worry, there is nothing to worry about' because we want to make things right for our for our children.

However, if your child is angry, worried, stressed or sad, the first step in giving them the confidence to deal with these feelings is to **help them understand what they are feeling and why**.

positive feelings
The most effective way to boost your child's inner confidence is to **encourage them to talk about their positive feelings**.

Focus on a **'feeling-finding' mission**. Make it a priority to encourage your child to talk about their positive feelings. What do **they** enjoy about their favourite sport or hobby or having great friends? Instead of talking to them about what **you think** they do well, talk about what **they think** they do well.

skill builder
the confidence connection

*When it comes to boosting confidence, the really important thing is for **you** to connect with **your child**. It is good for you – and it is great for them.*

1 boosting your child's confidence

Take a look at the confidence wheel below. Each segment contains something that you can do as a mum that will boost your child's confidence. You probably do most of these things without thinking.

How many of them have you done over the past 24 hours? Every 'Yes' answer means that you have done something to boost their confidence and make them feel secure.

Be there for them

Look into their eyes

Have fun with them

Listen to them

Make them feel valued

Tell them you love them

Cuddle them

Praise them

teenagers and toddlers both need confidence

When our children are younger, we tend to put these confidence-boosters into practice more often. But remember it is just as important to do all of them with a teenager as it is with a toddler.

2 do something new with your child

Each new day brings new challenges and new rewards– for you and your child. To them, each day is an adventure, full of new experiences. It is by constantly embracing new challenges that we grow and develop. Completing each new challenge gives us the confidence to take on the next.

Identify one activity that you and your child can learn to do together – and enjoy sharing the experience. For example, you can both go to yoga classes, go ice skating, learn to swim or dance, fly a kite, ride a bike, bake a cake, or take a thrilling roller coaster ride. There are plenty of opportunities. Choose something that you would both love to do together.

Put a date in your diary – and make it happen. Take a photo of what you do and put it in a room that you both use a lot. This will be a constant reminder of just how adventurous you are together and what a great team you make.

display that picture today
If you put a picture up on the day it happens, your child will know that you are attaching importance and value to it – and the time you've enjoyed with them.

3 visual confidence boosters

The time that you spend with your child is precious – and it goes so quickly. When exciting things happen – like their first word or first step – we often think we will remember them forever. But, of course, family life is so busy and exciting, with so many amazing things happening, that we forget.

Your child achieves a huge amount every day. Like most mums, you probably have piles of things they have made – pictures, cards, models. You may have a box with notes they have sent you or the first story they wrote, a swimming certificate, or a piece of schoolwork that their teacher has written a special comment on.

Just as it is good for us to be reminded about what we have done that we are proud of, it is really good for our child to do this too. One of the easiest and most powerful ways is to celebrate their achievements by displaying them around the house.

Sort through your piles and boxes and choose some special things to put up in the kitchen or living room, or in your bedroom or theirs. Involve them in the process and decide how to do it. You can stick them to doors with poster putty or on pinboards – or you could use clip frames, which are easy, look great on the walls and create an instant gallery.

It is great to look back on what they have achieved and how they felt about it – what was fun and exciting. Your child will love being surrounded by instant confidence-boosters.

troubleshooting

Your young son is starting school soon and you are really excited. You are getting more nervous as the first day approaches. You know there are going to be tears at the school gate – and they are most likely to be yours!

▶ The first day of school is an exciting and challenging time. Your mixed feelings are absolutely normal. Starting school is a big step and you want to handle it well. It is usually the mums who are anxious – their children are fine.

▶ Be a positive role model. If you are tense and nervous about your son's first day, he is more likely to be tense. If you treat it as an exciting adventure, he will treat it as an adventure as well. Set a good example in the playground too. Make an effort to mix with the other parents – even if you are shy. It will help your child develop his social skills.

▶ Focus on the qualities and skills your child has that will help him to enjoy school life and to be a good friend and a valued member of the community. We often tell our children we love them – now tell him exactly what you love about him. The more specific you are, the more you will boost his confidence and self-belief.

▶ Build your toddler's confidence in practical ways instead of worrying about reading, writing or numbers. Encourage him to develop independence when it comes to getting dressed. For example, being able to put on and take off his coat, shoes and socks will really help him at school.

Your children are always on the go and constantly asking you to let them join a new club or try out another after-school activity. You want to encourage them to develop a range of interests but you don't want them to end up doing too much.

▶ It is great to encourage your children to try new things. It boosts their confidence in building relationships and exposes them to a range of different characters and interests. The more you encourage them to talk about their positive feelings associated with the activity, the more their confidence and self-belief will grow. Just like learning an instrument, asking the right questions takes practice!

▶ It is also important to have a healthy balance. Saying 'Yes' to all extracurricular activities will make family life – for you and your children – more frantic and less fun. By encouraging your children to make decisions about how to spend their time and prioritize the activities they want to pursue, you are teaching them an important skill.

▶ You are a parent – not a taxi-driver – although it may not seem like it at times. It may seem fantastic to give your children the chance of an extra swimming lesson, but they may get more out of having a great time with you. Don't let the extracurricular activities control your family life. Children don't need to have things organized for them all the time. Put the family times you want to keep special in your diary and then organize any extra-curricular activities around them.

Your toddler has started nursery and his social life has really taken off. He is more in demand than you, with a party every couple of weeks. But you dread them. You know he is going to cling to you from the moment you arrive and scream if you leave his side.

▶ This is normal. Lots of toddlers feel this way. Parties can be daunting for little ones – and their mums. Think positive. If you go along to the party feeling tense, your toddler is more likely to feel the same way. If you are excited, he is likely to enjoy it more. Enlist the help of another mum and go along to the party together so that your toddler arrives with a friend.

▶ Help yourself stay calm by seeing the party through his eyes. Your toddler is learning to be independent and get to grips with a big new social world and that is a challenge.

▶ Try hard to ignore his clingy behaviour. Motivate him by praising him for playing and sharing with other children.

▶ Be a great role model. Make mixing with other mums and dads a real priority. Get chatting – at parties, at the nursery and in the park.

▶ Organize regular play dates with other toddlers. Introduce your toddler to a circle of friends, not just one. This will help him to develop confidence in social situations.

▶ Be a positive party-pooper. Life is about choices. Don't feel your toddler has to go to every party that he is invited to – do what works for you.

I am a motivating leader

You are your family's team leader and if you want to make something happen – you will. You will lead your family to achieve it. You have a vision and as you lead your team towards it, you are helping your child to develop and grow. Your own motivation is the key to your success and happiness as a mum. When you are motivated, you feel energized and positive. When you are demotivated, you feel strained and negative – and you stand still. The same is true of your child. And when it comes to motivating your son or daughter, you are the expert and you hold the key.

▶A **motivated** family is a **positive and energized** family

▶You are teaching **essential life skills**, especially when it comes to **resolving conflict**

▶You will **inspire** your child

motivating your family

You are your family's team leader. You are their captain. This is a role with big responsibilities. Your child is in your hands and you are walking with them into the future. You want them to enjoy the journey from childhood into adulthood, you want to nurture them and build their confidence – and you want them to have fun and feel secure.

what makes a great family team leader?

As a great team leader you will have vision and inspire and motivate your family. You will encourage your children to love and support each other and work together. You help them to resolve family conflict fairly and to understand and respect each other's points of view.

In this way, you are motivating them to live together as a family team. You know this will help you all to grow in many different ways. You know that a united family is strong and powerful – especially when it comes to facing life's challenges together.

motivation

Motivation is the key to a happy family and your success as team leader. As a mum, you will know how powerful it feels to be motivated – and just how draining it can feel to be demotivated. When it comes to your child, you are constantly called on to motivate them, especially when it comes to things they really don't want to do, such as tidying their bedroom, going to bed, eating vegetables or doing their homework.

You are already a good motivator. As your child grows, you learn to tune in to them. You have a great gut instinct about what makes them tick. You motivate them on a daily basis. The more effective you are, the easier your life will be and the happier and more positive you will all feel.

get the motivation balance right

There may be times when you just wish your child would do something without you having to think of ways of motivating them. This is a good lesson for them to learn too – but make it the exception not the rule. Healthy family life is all about getting a positive balance.

Research shows that the average mum says 'No' between 30 and 50 times a day. After a while, it can become a habit and you find yourself saying it without realizing. If you say 'No' too often, it loses its power. Focus today on how often you say 'No' and only say it when you **really mean it**. A good motivator says 'Yes' more often than 'No'.

the power of 'I want'

Feeling motivated is positive and energizing. Feeling demotivated is a negative and stressful experience.

There is a big difference in how you feel when it comes to what you **need** to do and what you **want** to do. You are likely to feel **less motivated** to achieve something that you **need** to do. On the other hand, you are likely to feel **more powerfully motivated** to achieve something that you **want** to do.

On the surface, one task may seem more urgent. However, in practice, you are more likely to do what you want to do rather than what you need to do because you are motivated to achieve it. If you need to do something, it will drain your energy and you will probably find all sorts of reasons for not doing it.

If you want to do something, you will feel energized. You will find reasons to make it happen. The same is true of your child – as you are probably very aware. If they really want to do something, they will make it happen.

lead from the front

A great family team leader knows her team and wants to nurture their children as individuals and as part of the team. She also recognizes her own strengths and weaknesses, is not afraid to delegate and is generous with praise where it is deserved.

1 know your team

Write down the names of the different members of your family team and focus on one at a time – including yourself. What does each person bring to the team in terms of personality, skills and qualities. Close your eyes and picture their faces as you enjoy celebrating all that is positive about them.

don't do it all – delegate

Good team leaders delegate. They don't do everything themselves just because it is easier or quicker. This is a short-term view and team leaders have long-term vision. You are taking your child on the journey to independence and the more you encourage them to take responsibility, the better it will be for all of you in the long run.

2 your role as team leader

Take a look at the leadership wheel below. It lists some examples of the qualities that help mums to be strong, positive and effective team leaders

Look at each of the qualities in turn and think about how good you are at each of them. Then ask yourself the following questions:

► Which area do you find most challenging?

► Which area do you perform best at?

► Which area would you like to focus on improving today?

By taking the time to prioritize where you are as a family team leader today – and where you want to be, you will be taking the first step to achieving your goal.

see things through your child's eyes

A good team leader will always take other people's views and feelings into account. Which quality do you think your child believes is your strongest?

3 praise your child for being part of the team

All members of your family will bring lots of things to the family team. Each one of you is an individual and this is what makes managing your team such an unpredictable adventure. Together you make a whole and together you are stronger.

start today

► **Focus more on the positive ways your family works as a team.** Sometimes we can take this for granted and let it go unnoticed. Or we focus on family arguments. Keep things in perspective.

► **Instead of pointing out the negatives**, give your child attention for the right reasons and praise their positive team-building behaviour. Whenever you catch any members of your family showing good team spirit, praise them for it. Be specific about what they have done well to help the family team and they will be more likely to do it again.

team-building ideas

Here are some suggestions to help build your team:

► Encourage older children to read to their younger siblings or cousins – they will all love it

► Let your child choose a dish for a family meal and have fun cooking it with you

► Play a team game, such as charades or ball games, or do a jigsaw together

► Ask everyone to say what they love best about their brother or sister or mum or dad

► Hold a family meeting and ask everyone to put something on the agenda. This is a good opportunity to tackle family issues, but be sure to include fun items, such as what to do at the weekend

assess your motivation skills

Before you can improve your motivational skills, you need to know how motivated you are at the moment and to identify the skills that you already have.

1 your motivation rating

Think about what motivates you. What is your motivation for committing time and energy to make positive changes in your life so that you can be the mum you want to be? Is this something that you feel you **need** to do – or something that you **want** to do?

How motivated do you feel to make these changes happen? **Give yourself a rating on a scale of 1 to 10** – where 10 indicates a high level of motivation and 1 indicates a low level of motivation.

If you understand what motivates you, it will help you to motivate your child.

it is better to give than to take

Sanctions can sometimes be effective in getting your child to behave in the way you want. However, they are not a positive, motivational tool and parents often get stressed when they have to issue them. Use them sparingly when you have tried everything else and don't let them become a habit. If you do, make sure you go through with it – say what you mean and mean what you say. Idle threats are worse than useless.

The majority of people – both children and adults – are more motivated by incentives than ultimatums. Think about how you feel when people threaten you or issue ultimatums. You feel negative and defensive. Then think about how you feel when you receive praise or privileges. You feel positive and dynamic. The same is true for your child.

It is always more effective to give something to your child – your time, praise, a treat or a privilege – than it is to take it away.

2 the motivation quiz

Take a look at the statements in the table below.
Score 1 mark for every statement you say 'Yes' to.

Motivational skill

▶ I know what motivates me

▶ I know what motivates my child

▶ I enjoy inspiring my child to do things they didn't think possible

▶ I help my child to set specific goals

▶ I encourage them to identify their own ways to achieve their goals

▶ I praise specific behaviour that I want to encourage

▶ I explain what to do instead of telling them what not to do

▶ I use alternatives to threats and ultimatums

▶ I can turn a 'need to' into a 'want to' when it comes to motivating my children

▶ I celebrate their achievements with them

how did you score?
0–3 marks You have the potential to be a motivating mum.
4–7 marks You display strong motivational skills.
8–10 marks Congratulations – you are a very motivating mum.

give your child choices
Your child may not be feeling motivated about something you want them to do – whether it is tidying their room or doing their homework. Try giving them a choice about the order they want to do the 'chores' in. In this way they will feel they are in the driving seat and are much more likely to make it happen.

3 life isn't about success and failure

One of the great demotivating forces at work in the world is the fear of failure. Many people judge themselves in terms of 'success' or 'failure'.

A much more motivating approach to life is to see it in terms of a learning experience. This means that even if things don't turn out the way you wanted or expected, you have still learnt something from the experience. It is often when we feel most challenged in life that we learn the most about ourselves and grow.

Help your child to understand that life isn't about success and failure. It is about growing as an individual and learning fresh ways to approach things.

how to help your children

▶ Be a great role model and adopt this approach in your own life

▶ Stop using the language of failure yourself

▶ Tune into their failure language and challenge it

▶ When things don't turn out as they want, help them to see it from a positive perspective

▶ When one idea doesn't work, encourage them to think of another one instead of giving up

be the motivator you want to be

Every mum will do things their own way – and so she should. You are the expert and your child is unique. What works for one mum just doesn't work for another. Life is about choices and making decisions that work for you and your family. Go with your gut instinct – and you will be proved absolutely right.

1 be specific with your praise

Praise is a very powerful motivational tool. Your child loves your attention and the best way for them to get it is by you praising them. As a mum, you are probably great at praising your child already but it is still useful to **focus on the ways you use praise** to make it even more effective.

It can be easy to find something to praise in a toddler, but praising your tweenie and teenager is just as essential – even if you have to work a bit harder to do it.

the golden rules for praise
▶ Be on the lookout – don't let good behaviour go unnoticed
▶ Be specific
▶ Be consistent
▶ Be tactile and praise with a kiss and cuddle as well as words

Put these into practice today!

facts about praise
- 9 out of 10 mums say they frequently praise their toddlers
- 7 out of 10 mums say they frequently praise their 'tweenies'
- 3 out of 10 mums say they frequently praise their teenagers

2 rewards and treats – bribery or incentive?

Every mum will have her own opinion about giving treats to her child as a reward for certain behaviours. One mum's incentive is another mum's bribe. Some mums like to use praise alone. Many find star charts with rewards work well. Some use time, privileges or toys. What is important is that you have thought about what **you want to do**.

Use your creativity and initiative to think outside the box when it comes to rewards. Your child doesn't even think there is a box!

Many mums find it helpful to use screen time as an incentive – a reward that is earned – rather than something that their children do anyway and take for granted. Focusing on screen time in a positive way can help you as a mum to ensure that you stay in control and help your children to value their screen time more.

the golden rules for screen time

▶ Be calm – screens can bring out the worst in mums

▶ Be clear – agree exactly what you want your children to do, how many minutes of screen time it will earn them and when they can take it

▶ Be specific – decide when they can 'cash in' their screen time

▶ Be open – encourage their input into creating a system that works

▶ Be simple – set up a system that is easy to put into action

Another way of giving your child an incentive is to **issue a challenge**. Children love to prove their mums wrong and it can be really effective to say things like 'I'm sure you won't be able to put all of your toys in the toy box before I count to 10'.

facts about motivation

- *8 out of 10 mums use screen time – such as watching TV, time on the computer or playing video games – as a reward*
- *6 out of 10 mums use privileges – such as staying up late or having a friend around*
- *3 out of 10 mums use time with mum – such as going out, swimming or playing together*

3 keep a family fun file

Having fun together is the best possible family team-building exercise you can ever do. It will motivate and energize you all.

Start a family fun file full of ideas about what the family can have fun doing together. Ask everyone to contribute an idea – and keep your eyes open for articles in papers and magazines and include recommendations from other families.

Make it even more interesting by asking your family to suggest something you have never done together before. Put the ideas into a hat and pull them out one at a time. Put them in your diary – and make them happen.

troubleshooting

You broke up with your partner over a year ago. Now you have met someone else and you are very happy. You want your daughter to meet him and his children but you are worried about how she will react.

▶ This is a big step for all of you. You are asking yourself all the right questions. Go with your gut instinct and it will be spot on.

▶ Don't fall into the trap of worrying about potential problems. Instead, write down all the benefits that the three of you will get out of spending time together.

▶ Take this one step at a time. It will help you all to feel positive, relaxed and focused. Arrange for your daughter to meet your new partner first and his family later.

▶ It may be best to make the first meeting somewhere neutral and away from home. Get your daughter excited about the date with mum and her new friend. Get her input and give her some choices about where she would like to go.

▶ After your successful first meeting, give your daughter a big cuddle as you put her to bed and share what you have both enjoyed about the day. Also talk to your new partner about how you are feeling and what you can both do to help and support each other. He is probably feeling nervous too!

You are worried about your partner's health. He is in a stressful job and has an unhealthy lifestyle. You want to help him to get into shape now that he has a young family, but you don't want to nag.

▶ Lots of mums worry about their own and their partner's health. You want to be as healthy and energetic as possible so you can get the most out of family life. Set a good example. If you are positive, healthy and motivated, your husband is more likely to want to be too.

▶ Get out of the habit of looking at your partner and seeing the things about him that you want to change. Instead, look at him and focus on the things you love about him and what a great dad he is. Tell him – it will help him to feel positive about himself.

▶ You can't change your partner. He has to want to change himself. He is much more likely to do it if he is motivated. Talk to him about what you both enjoy about being parents. Identify some great physical family activities you can all enjoy together, such as swimming, cycling or tennis. Book an activity – and do it.

▶ Help him cut his stress levels by talking to him about life in terms of solutions, not problems.

You are a first-time mum. Your partner works all day during the week then would rather play on the computer than spend time with your daughter. You want to know if this is normal and what you can do to change it.

▶ Being parents marks the beginning of a new chapter in your relationship and you will learn to adapt as you deal with the challenges of family life.

▶ It is normal for some dads to respond to the demands of fatherhood by locking themselves away. Being a dad is a huge responsibility and many dads say they lack confidence, don't know what to do and are worried about failing. They often believe that mums are the experts – not them.

▶ Your partner may be unsure about what to do, so be specific about the things you would like him to help you with. Praise him for what he does well as a dad. This will boost his confidence.

▶ Encourage him to enjoy dad–child bonding time. Let him choose an activity that he wants to do and leave him to it. He may like to do something that involves another dad. They can support each other.

▶ You can't wave a magic wand and change your partner but, by being positive and taking it a step at a time, you can give him the confidence and motivation to change himself.

I am a feel-good mum

You know just how great you feel when you are on top of the world and enjoying your child. You also know that the demands of family life can lead to strong negative feelings that you struggle to deal with. The most powerful negative feeling, which mums say they find the hardest to cope with, is guilt. It is important to deal with feelings of guilt. They have a huge impact on you and your child. If you leave guilty feelings to fester, they will just grow stronger. As a mum, you have lots to feel good about and this chapter will help you to deal with the negative feelings and invest your energy in a positive way.

▶ You will have a **healthier** and **happier** mind, body and soul

▶ Life is **too short to waste time** feeling guilty

▶ If you **feel good about yourself**, your child will **feel good about themselves**

the power
of guilt

Guilt is a really powerful feeling. Think about the word and the images that come to mind when you say it. Guilt is something you usually associate with criminals, law courts or prison – not with mums bringing up children. So why do mums put themselves in the dock and find themselves guilty on so many counts? They have committed no crime. On the contrary, they are working hard to be the best mums they can.

The only person who can reduce your feelings of guilt is you. This is very liberating because it means you can take control and do something about it if you want to.

The actual process of feeling guilty does nothing to help. The more time you spend thinking about it or talking about it, the more guilty you will feel. It reinforces the powerful negative messages you are sending to yourself and all around you.

The way to reduce guilt is to think positive and to take action to replace those negative feelings with positive ones.

the limiting effect of guilt

Feeling guilty doesn't only affect you and your happiness. It also has an impact on the whole family. While you are spending time feeling guilty, you aren't spending time being the mum you want to be. It limits you and it limits your family life.

all mums feel guilty

If you are a working mum, you may be struggling to combine family life with a demanding career. Your stress levels are high and your energy levels are low. You are giving everything you have got and it still isn't enough. But that isn't the worst of it. You are also wrestling with sometimes overwhelming feelings of guilt as you try to perform at work and at home and feel you are failing at both.

However, guilt doesn't just affect mums in paid employment. All mums are working mums. Full-time mums report that they often feel guilty too because they don't always enjoy all the time they spend with their children. They say they can feel negative and frustrated.

note to self

Focus on the positive aspects of being a mum. Don't let negative thoughts overpower positive thoughts. By focusing on the positive, I will boost my feel-good factor and reduce my feel-guilty factor.

thinking negative +
taking no action =
feeling guilty

thinking positive +
taking action =
feeling good

the guilt gremlin

You create your own guilt gremlin. You give him strength. He sits there on your shoulder, whispering in your ear because he knows that he has your attention. He talks ugly. He knows exactly what to say to hit the spot and make you feel dreadful. He is at his most powerful when you are feeling vulnerable. He is strongest when you are at your weakest.

The tell-tale signs of a feel-guilty mum are:

▶ Talking a lot about guilt – wearing the T-shirt and having the DVD

▶ Not fulfilling her potential because the feelings of guilt hold her back

▶ Spending money on her child to make herself feel better

take yourself out of the dock today

Today is the day to commit yourself to stop wasting valuable time feeling guilty and to start investing it in positive thoughts and actions. As a mum you are probably an expert at making yourself feel guilty but not so great at letting yourself feel good. You are like all mums – you give yourself a hard time on a daily basis and rarely acknowledge what you achieve.

It is time to take yourself out of the dock. Your time with your child is far too precious to waste feeling guilty. Take the first step by spending your time focusing on what makes you feel good about being a mum instead of what makes you feel guilty.

think positive and take action

The majority of mums feel guilty. Guilt goes with the job. If you want to deal with your feelings of guilt, think positive, use positive language, identify what makes you feel guilty and take action.

1 talk 'good' not 'guilty'

Stop using the language of guilt. Don't talk about feeling guilty or what you haven't or should have done. The more you talk about it, the worse you will feel. Talking about it paralyses you and you stand still. Rise to the challenge today – talk about what makes you feel good as a mum and what has gone well – and encourage other mums to do the same.

get rid of guilt

Whenever you feel your guilt gremlin rear its ugly head, cuddle your child – or close your eyes and picture them – and focus on all the reasons you have to feel good about being a mum. Say out loud 'I feel good about being a mum' – and believe it.

2 identify what makes you feel guilty

In order to deal with your feelings of guilt it is important to **break down the big picture and focus on the specific causes of these feelings.** The more specific you are about the problem, the more effective you will be in finding a solution.

Look at the guilt wheel below and you will see examples of the most common situations that mums identify as causing them most guilt.

Read them carefully and focus on the one that is making you feel the most guilty and that you would like most to do something about. There may be another situation that is specific to you, in which case, focus on this.

Once you have identified what you want to focus on, **think about it in more detail.** What exactly is it that causes you to feel guilty? Be as specific as you can.

YOUR IDEA

Being at work instead of with my child

Child crying when left with child minder

Taking 'me' time

Missing my child's bedtimes, mealtimes, etc.

Neglecting my partner

Being negative when with my child

Being too stressed to be a fun mum

3 decide what to do

The big question now is one that only you can answer. **What is the one practical thing you can do – which is within your control – that will help to reduce your feelings of guilt in your chosen area?** Think hard. You will have the answers but you probably haven't yet given yourself the time to focus on them.

Look at the table below, which gives examples of the actions that you could take to deal with the situations on the guilt wheel. However, it is always better to use your own ideas.

Causes of guilt	Action
Being at work instead of with my child	Write down the benefits to your child of spending time in the company of other adults and children
Child crying when left with child minder or at nursery	Arrange an appointment with the child minder and develop a new joint action plan. Remember – you are a team.
Missing my child's bedtimes, mealtimes, etc	Leave work on time at least once a week
Too stressed to be a fun mum	Learn a meditation technique that you can put into practice at home
Neglecting my partner	Book a babysitter and go on a date together
Taking 'me' time	Recognize that 'me' time is vital if you are going to be the best mum you can be – and book a massage!

Action always brings about changes. If you keep doing the same things, nothing will change. By taking action, you will be taking a positive step in the right direction.

skill builder
say goodbye to guilt

There may be a lot of positive feelings that you would like to be experiencing in place of those feelings of guilt. Boost these positive feelings and you will find that the guilty feelings have less impact.

1 the 24-hour positive-feeling booster

Look at the table below, which lists some of the most common positive feelings that mums say they would like to have more of and examples of the actions that could be taken to achieve them.

Decide which one positive feeling you would most like to boost in your life over the next 24 hours and write down the actions that you would take to help you achieve it. Think simple. The easier it is to do, the more likely you are to do it.

Positive feeling	Examples of actions
Good	Do one thing today that you have been putting off for ages
Positive	Count your blessings and share them with your child
Relaxed	Take a long soak in the bath with candles
At peace	Write down three things that you do well as a mum
Energized	Go for a brisk walk or bike ride with your child
Happy	Cuddle your children and tell them a story
Fun	Draw faces on your child's feet with your finger and make everyone laugh
Other	Your own idea

Once you have decided what you want to do – go ahead and do it. Enjoy catching yourself feeling good or positive, calm, relaxed or at peace, or energized, happy or fun. By focusing on what you want to achieve, you will notice a difference – and so will your child.

2 be positive about the time you spend apart

It is easy to understand why mums feel guilty about being away from their children. However, this negative feeling often takes control so that you struggle to see your situation from any other perspective.

In practice, although you will still have the usual challenges to contend with, there will be positive benefits to your children in spending their time in the company of other adults and children.

see your time apart as a win-win situation

Look at the situation positively and think about the benefits to every one of you.

▶ Write down the greatest single benefit to you about spending time away from your child

▶ Write down the greatest benefit to your child about spending time away from you

facts about feeling good
- *9 out of 10 working mums say the financial security gives their children opportunities that would not otherwise be possible*
- *9 out of 10 mums say successfully combining family and work helps them to feel more complete as a person*
- *9 out of 10 mums say they appreciate their children much more when they are with them*
- *8 out of 10 mums say nursery helps their children develop strong social skills*

be positive about childcare

Don't let your imagination run riot by convincing yourself that your children are unhappy because you are not with them. They will benefit from mixing with other people and will take part in a range of activities you may never do with them. Put a picture of them laughing on your desk. Look at it often.

3 boost your energy

Guilt thrives in tired and stressed mums. **Make sure that you have enough energy to cope.** Whether you are at home or at work, make sure that you:

▶ Eat breakfast

▶ Drink plenty of water

▶ Eat healthy snacks, including fruit and vegetables

▶ Take a lunch break

▶ Get at least 10 minutes fresh air during the day

Recognize that taking time to nurture yourself and boost your energy levels benefits the whole family as well as yourself. In this way, you will be a really strong role model to your child and they will be much more likely to develop healthy habits themselves.

troubleshooting

You feel hurt because your son seems to prefer his child minder to you. When you go to pick him up after work, he cries and doesn't want to leave. She is great but you feel guilty because he seems to like her more than you.

Dealing with the guilt and stress that comes from juggling work and family life is one of the toughest challenges you will have to face.

Focus on the positives about your situation. You have made a good decision and chosen a child minder whom you and your child both really like. Praise your child minder. It is important to recognize that the negative feelings you have about the situation are about you – not about him.

Resolve to leave work on time. If you are late and rushing from work to your child minder, you will feel tense.

You and your child minder aren't competitors for your son's attention – you are a team. If you arrive there dreading the pick-up, it is much more likely to be a negative experience for all of you. Arrive today, looking forward to seeing him and committed to feeling relaxed and enjoying the experience.

Your time may be limited in the evenings but remember that, no matter how much he loves the child minder, nobody ever compares to mum!

You are finding nursery drop-offs really difficult. The drive there is a nightmare and your toddler screams when you leave. His key worker is great and tells you that he is fine within minutes – but you feel guilty all day.

▶ The dreaded nursery drop-off can strike fear into the heart of the strongest mum. There is nothing worse than leaving your toddler when he is screaming – especially in front of other mums.

▶ Don't make life difficult for yourself by rushing out of the door at the last possible moment. Leave with time to spare and enjoy the journey more.

▶ Don't let your imagination run wild. Your son is happy at the nursery. His key worker tells you that he is fine – and he is. Surround yourself with happy photos – on your desk, on the fridge, in your bag – and remind yourself that he really does have this much fun at nursery too.

▶ It is tough but stay strong. At the moment your son is controlling you. He knows that he will get your attention when he cries. But the more attention you give him for screaming, the more he will scream.

▶ Arrange a meeting with his key worker and develop a new plan of action together.

You have just returned to work after having your first baby and your stress levels have hit an all-time high. You are thrilled about being a mum, and you used to enjoy your job, but now you feel guilty because you are failing at both.

▶ Every working mum knows how stressful it is to juggle family and work, especially if you are doing it for the first time. Life as a working mum is about compromise and about doing the best you can do – not about being perfect. It is about taking small steps to get the balance that you want – and taking each small step is a massive achievement.

▶ Make life as easy as you can for yourself. Cut down on ironing, switch on the answering machine, hide the vacuum cleaner, stock up with ready-made meals and order shopping online.

▶ Find out whether your employer runs a parent support network. Get together with other mums and there will be many ways to help each other.

▶ When you are at work, enjoy yourself. There are real benefits to being a working mum – for you as an individual and for your family.

▶ Believe in yourself. Employers say that employees become even more creative, productive and resourceful once they have a family. And your baby thinks you are the best thing in the world.

I am the mum I want to be

You are a mum who is investing time and energy to be the mum you want to be to your child. You are committed to developing your parenting skills because you know it is the most important job you will ever do in your life. That makes you exceptional. You want your child to grow up being the person that they want to be and making their own decisions about their lives. You don't want them to grow up living a life that other people tell them to live. You want them to have that robust inner confidence and self-belief to live their own lives to the full – in the way they want to lead them.

▶You show your child that they can **be the person they want to be** too

▶You will **achieve your real potential** as a parent

▶Because **you can**!

be a pioneer – raise a pioneer

As mentioned in Chapter 1, as a mum, you are a pioneer and your son or daughter will always follow in your footsteps. The more pioneering you are, the more pioneering they will be. The more you take responsibility for your life and enjoy the adventure, the more they will do so. If your child sees you enjoying being the mum you want to be, they are much more likely to grow up being the person they want to be.

note to self

*I am the only person who can stop myself from being the mum I want to be and the only person who can ensure that I am the mum I want to be. It is tough and I will have to work at it on a daily basis – but I **can** make it happen.*

By creating time in your busy day to read this book and using the skill-building strategies, you will have made significant moves towards your goal. Every day you are taking a step closer to your destination.

Often you have so many things to think about as a mum that the challenges can seem overwhelming. There can be so much to deal with that it is hard to get around to doing anything about any of them.

You are different. You have successfully **broken down the big picture** in order to **focus on specific areas** of family life, to **prioritize what you want to achieve** and to **commit to an action plan to achieve it**.

You have demonstrated all the qualities of the mum you want to be and you are now ready to sign the contract.

being a mum is your most important lesson in life

It seems strange that, in our society, we take lessons or go to classes to learn how to drive, swim, play tennis or get fit. But, as a mum, the most important job you will do in your life, it is really down to you. You have children and they come with no instructions – and you are expected to know what to do with them and how to do it.

By reading this book and putting the ideas into practice, you have taken the initiative. You are driving yourself and your family forward.

the big picture

Being a mum is a unique experience. As we near the end of this journey together, it is a good time to reflect on the big picture.

Your child is like a blank canvas – and you are the passionate and talented artist. You have the skills and the tools to create a masterpiece. As a mum, you can add energy and colour, vibrancy and depth, and meaning and love to that picture on a daily basis.

Your child is the sum of all the time and energy you invest in them and the love you give them – the laughs you have shared, the kisses and cuddles, the fun you have had, the challenges you have overcome, the books you have read, your trips out together, family holidays, and always being there for them.

The more successful you are at being the mum you want to be, the greater your masterpiece will be.

you can do it

The key to your success is **you**. If you want to do it – you will do it. It is tough and you will work at it on a daily basis. But you can make it happen and – just like childbirth – the rewards will always outweigh the effort.

Remember:

▶ Always go with your gut instinct – it will be right

▶ Do what **you** want to do – not what other people tell you to do or what you think you ought to do

▶ Acknowledge that you are the expert and know what is best for your child

▶ Focus on what **you** think – not what other people think

▶ Follow your heart

▶ Believe in yourself

'I am the mum I want to be' contract

▶ I have vision.

▶ I am inspiring.

▶ I am motivated.

▶ I make good decisions.

▶ I am strong.

▶ I am energetic.

▶ I am positive.

▶ I believe in myself.

▶ I am committed to being the mum I want to be.

Signature...

Date...

picture your dreams and aspirations

You may think about your child's dreams and aspirations but it is important to have your own dreams and aspirations as well. By working towards them, you are in the very best situation to help your child achieve dreams as well.

help your child achieve their dreams

As their mum, you are the person who can walk with your child on their journey to adulthood and help them to turn their dreams and aspirations into a reality. Enjoy creating those dreams and aspirations with them and walking each step with them.

1 make your own montage

Create a visual goal in terms of the mum you want to be by making a picture montage. Whenever you read a paper or magazine and see an image that reminds you of the mum you want to be, tear it out and stick it on to your 'mum montage'.

The examples below show some of the qualities you may aspire to and what you could use to remind you of them:

▶ Calm – a picture of the sea or a sunset

▶ Energetic – a picture of an athlete or footballer you admire

▶ Fun – a colour or an image that represents fun to you, or a cartoon

▶ Adventurous – a picture of a mountain or an adventure holiday advertisement

▶ Inspirational – an image of someone you find inspirational, or a quote

If you see any words that describe what you would like to be, add them to your montage.

Look at your montage every night before you go to bed. By focusing on the mum you want to be and being specific about the destination you want to reach, you are bringing those dreams one step closer to becoming a reality.

Encourage your child to help you. Children love visual stimulation – and anything that involves mess and glue – so this is a great activity to involve them in. Talk to your child about the images you are choosing and what makes them important to you. It is a fantastic opportunity for you to talk to them about your aspirations and dreams – with pictures to illustrate them. Encourage your child to get involved by looking through magazines to find pictures that will help you – or by drawing pictures for you.

2 picture your child's dreams and aspirations

Encourage your child to talk about their dreams and aspirations and to make a colourful montage of their own. They will have great fun doing this.

Encourage them to think outside the box when it comes to choosing images. For example, ask them:

▶ What colour would they like to be and why?

▶ What 'wow' words (adjectives) would they use to describe themselves?

▶ Which sportsperson or superhero would they like to be?

▶ What animal would they like to be?

3 take your own advice

Visualize yourself in the future. Relax, close your eyes and imagine yourself in 20, 30 or 40 years from now. You are enjoying being a grandmother; your child has grown up and now has happy children of their own. You are together as a family – your team.

Imagine the scene as vividly as you can. Picture the vibrant colour and the faces of everyone around you. Think about how you look, what you are thinking and how you feel. Imagine what you are all talking about.

If you could pass on **one tip** to your child about being a parent, what would that tip be? **Say it out loud and write it down.** Take that advice yourself.

pass on your life lessons

The years go by so quickly. Time is short and before long your child will leave home and start to lead an independent life. You may think that day is a long way off – but it is racing towards you like an express train.

1 choose a lesson for your child

Focus on your child and what you want to help them achieve in their lives. Think of the many lessons that you have learnt during your lifetime – as a child, as an adult and, most particularly, as a mum.

What is the one key 'life' lesson that you really want them to learn from you and carry in their heart always? **Draw a heart, write this lesson on it and give it to them.**

2
write your child a love letter

Take precious time to write a note to your child, listing the reasons why you love them and what you love about being their mum. You will have your own style and you will know what you want to say. Here are some thoughts to get you started:

▶ How you felt when you first saw your baby

▶ How you feel every time you see them for the first time each day

▶ What your favourite memory is as a mum

▶ What you love most about your child – be specific and tell them the reasons

▶ What you enjoy doing together that makes you both laugh

▶ How you feel when you cuddle them

▶ What you have learnt from them

▶ How being a mum has helped you to grow in ways that would be impossible without children

▶ What you value most about your relationship with your child

▶ What they can do better than you – and you would like them to help you with

▶ What challenges they have embraced that have made you proud of them

You can keep adding to your letter whenever you want to.

what to do with the letters

▶ Read it to your child – they will never tire of hearing it

▶ Give the letters to your child on a special day – it will be a present that they will treasure forever

▶ Frame the letter and put them up in the house

▶ Record them on CD or DVD

This letter will be a gift that will last a lifetime.

3
create memories that will last forever

You are in a lifelong commitment with your child.

Close your eyes and focus on the future. Imagine you are sitting down talking to your child, who has now grown up with a family of their own. What will they remember from their childhood years? What great memories did you create that will stay with them for ever.

Choose three memories that you would like to create that your child will value forever.

You are a mum who writes her own life script. If these are the memories that you want your child to have – you are the person who can make them happen.

Every day your love will make a positive difference to your child. You are on the most important journey of your life. Take family life one step at a time –- and enjoy the adventure.

my child's memory box

memory 1   memory 2   memory 3

index

acknowledgements

With thanks to the special people who have made my book possible.

My agent Liz for her vision and my editor Jane at Hamlyn for her creativity and expertise. Roy, Keith, Ken and everyone in my brilliant family. Sophie, Angus, Rozi, Brian, Megumi and Antony for always being there for Josh and Holly. Tree for her brilliant ideas. Gill for her laughter and zest for life. Sarah for being the mum I want to be when I grow up. Elaine for her inspiration. Mum and dad for always believing in me. Josh and Holly for all of their love and laughter and for making me the happiest mum in the world. Ben for being awesome. Jerry for his love.

And, of course, all of the parents I have had the privilege to coach.

Executive Editor **Jane McIntosh**
Editor **Ruth Wiseall**
Executive Art Editor **Penny Stock**
Designer **Miranda Harvey**
Senior Production Controller **Linda Parry**
Picture Researcher **Taura Riley**

Photography: Alamy/Picture Partners 30. Corbis/Bloomimage 62, 124; Fancy/Veer 78. Fotolia/kzenon 96. Getty Images/AAGAMIA 112; altrendo images 28, 42, 107; amana productions inc 60; Andreas Brandt 102; DCA Productions 46; John-Francis Bourke 2; Jose Luis Pelaez Inc 11, 100, 100; Kane Skennar 71; Paul Burns 64; Tetra Images 18. Masterfile 12, 66, 108, 110, 114; Mark Leibowitz 51; Noel Hendrickson 4; Rolf Bruderer 76, 83, 84. moodboard 38, 58, 72, 74, 52. Octopus Publishing Group Limited/Russell Sadur 14, 16, 24, 35, 40, 88, 94, 98. Photolibrary/Banana Stock 36; stockybyte 23. Punchstock/Blend Images 86. Shutterstock/Arne Trautmann 120; Monkey Business Images 26, 122. Tips Images Ltd 54, 90.